"The poems in this superb collection by Harold J. Recinos are testaments to that lifeforce he calls the 'wondrous human river.' In exquisite lines and sentences, lucid images, and passionate meditations on a contemporary culture 'voluptuous with hypocrisy,' Recinos returns his readers to the difficult, necessary, and ultimately beautiful work of building a multicultural America. In a time of rhetorical bluster and easy abstraction, here instead is the genuine imprint of humanity."

—Peter Campion
Author of *Radical as Reality: Form and Freedom in American Poetry*

"This collection of poetry is spiritual manna for our time. Harold J. Recinos reminds us again and again of the potential of our humanity and the need for humility as we struggle to make our society a place of plenty for all. Recinos, the poet and theologian, is creating a new way to speak. In short, *The Place across the River* is holy."

—Lori Marie Carlson
Author of *A Path to the World: Becoming You*

"The richness, uniqueness, and legacy of Ibero-Indigeno-Africano Humanism soars in this new collection by Harold Recinos. Undergirded by an abiding, radical Christian faith, *The Place across the River* transports the hyper-situatedness of the dispossessed, the alienated, the refugee, the forgotten, the cursed, into a Cathedral of Light, whose dazzling poems splash us with the conviction needed to elevate our sense of justice and social transformation."

—Rodrigo Toscano
Author of *The Cut Point*

"The poems in Harold J. Recinos' *The Place across the River* read like beautiful, cinematic vignettes from the life of book-loving Puerto Rican boy coming of age, first in the music- and poetry-filled immigrant neighborhoods of New York City and later in the complicated and troubled landscapes of the United States. Recinos' poems memorialize as they bear witness, seek wonder as they critique, and, most of all, celebrate as they testify."

—FAISAL MOHYUDDIN
Author of *The Displaced Children of Displaced Children*

"Harold Recinos weaves a tapestry of sorrowful, joyful, glorious, and luminous mysteries through the pages of this remarkable collection of poems which read as prayers, capturing beauty and tragedy in the ordinary, and turning mundane moments into extraordinary revelations. This book is a testament to the enduring power of poetry to reflect on the death and miraculous being held together."

—TERESA DELGADO
Author of *A Puerto Rican Decolonial Theology: Prophesy Freedom*

The Place across the River

The Place across the River

HAROLD J. RECINOS

RESOURCE *Publications* · Eugene, Oregon

THE PLACE ACROSS THE RIVER

Copyright © 2024 Harold J. Recinos. All rights reserved. Except for brief quotations in critical publications or reviews, no part of this book may be reproduced in any manner without prior written permission from the publisher. Write: Permissions, Wipf and Stock Publishers, 199 W. 8th Ave., Suite 3, Eugene, OR 97401.

Resource Publications
An Imprint of Wipf and Stock Publishers
199 W. 8th Ave., Suite 3
Eugene, OR 97401

www.wipfandstock.com

paperback isbn: 979-8-3852-0326-0
hardcover isbn: 979-8-3852-0327-7
ebook isbn: 979-8-3852-0328-4

version number 011224

Contents

Beauty	1
Lovely	2
Hudson River	3
Ars Poetica	4
The Skillet	5
Hands	6
Slip Covers	7
Child	8
Trash	9
Last Night	10
Street Vendor	11
Harlem Hospital	12
April 7, 1985	13
Stupidity	14
The Philosopher	16
Street Fair	17
American Dream	18
Love Song	19
The Garden	20
Crucified	21

Reverse Bible	22
Morning	23
Detox	24
Throwaway Kid	26
End-time	28
Patriot Front March	29
Insurrection	30
The Ride	31
Barrio	32
El Paso	33
Meditation	35
Park Bench	36
The Crossing	37
The Valley	38
The Hammock	39
East Harlem	41
Long Island	42
The Massacre	43
Deadly Sins	45
Town Hall	46
Delicate	47
Collect Pond Park	48
Seasoning	49
Father	50
The Road	51
Darling	53
Woman	54
Restless	55
Junkie Boy	56

Revelation	58
Short	59
Colossal Silence	60
Congas	61
Dream	62
Old Woman	63
Sweetheart	64
Borrowed	65
Easter	66
The Projects	67
The Return	68
Woke	69
Stranger	70
Time for Woke	71
Books	72
Covenant School	73
Nazareth	74
Listen	75
No Passport	76
The Riverbank	78
Savior	79
Peace	80
Memory	81
Street Market	82
The Heights	83
Graveyard	84
Clang	85
Rio Grande	86
Jesus	87

The Martyr	88
Weary	89
The Laborers	90
Peace	91
Remember	92
Maundy Thursday	93
The Passion	94
Sidewalk	95
Risen	96
Waiting	97
Language Class	98
Prayer	99
Liar	100
Native Land	101
Night	102
Reality	103
Pray Tell	104
The Radio	105
Girlfriends	106
The Daughters	107
The Beginning	108
Spring Prayer	109
The Walk	110
Night Journey	111
Sanctuary	112
The Movies	113
Genesis	114
Lost Boy	115
Peace	116

The Messiah	117
The Poets	118
The Word	120
Evil	121
The Drunk	122
Love	123
The Preacher	124
Civil War	125
Crotona Park	126
Proud Mary	127
Dementia	128
Sofa Bed	129
Memorial Day	131
The Chevy	132
Subway Ride	133
The Beginning	134
Heal	135
La Placita	136
The Shore	137
Imago Dei	138
Torn Fabric	139
School Days	140
Locked	141
Church of All Nations	142
The Sneakers	143
The Living	144
The Professor	145
Sunday	146
Parsifal	147

Dawn	148
Looking	149
Witness	150
The Blues	152
Sage	153
Washington Square	154
The Crossing	155
Cruel Thing	156
Butterfly	157
Indictment	158
Word	159
The Subway	160
Chuck	161
The Cornerstone	162

BEAUTY

the evening on the museum steps
was a thing of mysterious beauty
like honey dripping from leaves
on old trees. I sat there observing
the parade of multicolored people
on the wide avenue, some calling
to each other, a few holding hands,
stepping off the curb laughing and
children too taking Herculean jumps
from the steps. I found majesty here,
in the noise of the city, the blaring of
sirens, honking horns and faces with
eager eyes. I was fully possessed by
the attractive scene and could almost
hear Angels blowing bugles from the
rooftop of the Art Museum leading me
to marvel deeply at God's art strolling
the sidewalks leaving aside the twisted
world if even for a single night.

LOVELY

your newly cut hair was wet
like rain with a loveliness no
simpler. morning air gathered
around you to make the sweet
hour from which words poured
out of you shine. I understood
the bird songs after all and they
swore in their musical way you
were a delicious sign of Eden.
I do now know love sinks deeper
than memory and when not a word
is left will be in us.

HUDSON RIVER

I walked across the bridge with
the broken English mothers who
wanted to see the Hudson River.
they wondered what it would be
like to swim in it, to make their way
down to the holy banks to be baptized
again by a Pentecostal pastor from
Brazil with the storefront, to walk wooded
paths beside it listening for decades-
old voices that never rot like leaves
and descend into dust. this ancient
river putting smiles on these mothers'
faces will never stop offering exquisite
dreams to make barrio women like them
speak in the mixed language of their new
world. we completed the long walk to the
other side of the bridge, made our way
down to the riverbank, placed naked feet
into the chilly water, then picked up stones
that managed without mouths to speak.

ARS POETICA

words wander at night to say
what they mean with simple
truth. they demand a hearing,
they possess me, they know me
and oblige me to claim them my
own. I tremble thinking they may
not speak some truth or reflect even
small images of history. these words
make blank white paper live and fill
empty spaces with things. with words I
leave the windows cracked just enough
to climb outside, have a look around the
block, skip on the streets and holler to
the Maker of meaning in sounds. words
are precious like life on the earth, hearing
birds sing and noticing neglected, loathed
and excluded things.

THE SKILLET

at night, by the wood fire beneath
the Comal toasting pupusas for a
shared meal, the mango tree leaves
moved by the wind, you bawling out
the prayers of the Rosary against war,
I swore darkness was approaching us
with thousands of intriguing dreams. we
thought heaven possessed us, believed
in the silence like mystics and thought
we heard the moon slowly drift over the
penniless house. not a single tear defiled
the petitions offered in the name of the
hope God completely knows for the sake
of the wretched on earth.

HANDS

last night we held hands until
finding the breach in the Wall,
the broken door inviting us in,
the place lonely spirits from
miles around come to whisper
in the dark and disable asylum.
we spent hours dreaming on the
Mexican side of the line, kneeling
for a time to pray your Rosary tucked
in the only bag you carried with a few
personal things, pictures of the dead
and missing. your face was more precious
than the twinkling sky, your braids far
more magical than Rapunzel's hair and
love was in you for me to see. we walked
through the hole like waking from a long
sleep and I was certain of entering a dream
untouched by sadness.

SLIP COVERS

the apartments had linoleum
floors people called carpet,
furniture was bought new then
dressed with custom made plastic
slip covers to keep things clean,
a television wore a wire hanger
whisker to provide reception good
enough for God's dithering attention
and a few framed pictures decorated
living room walls. the children
who lived in the place were born
small in history, learned to speak
Spanish until no longer needing it
for school to read Melville's story
of Ishmael and a Whale. little Rosa
spent each day jotting defiant things
down in a notebook that described
signs of beauty rejected by the warring
factions in the white world. a candle
always flickered in the apartment for
the dead, travelers, revolutionaries,
Saints and those held together in the
universe conjured in the night rooms
of the slum.

CHILD

brown child warmed by the sun made happy by the twisting wind blowing off the Hudson River to untangle your hair, completed by the precious maize that journeyed from North to South thanks to the hands of dark-skinned mothers that brought this radiant seed to the finest and humblest tables what do you pray with that Rosary? brown child hanging smiles in the air, staring at the far bank of the river, full of direction from the hurt villages of the poor, the dangerous coffee orchards, the bloody sugarcane fields, the hard labor of these northern lands making thousands weep how long will you sit there surrounded by sounds from the city waiting to get a look at what holds heaven up? brown child sitting by the river carried here so many years ago from a land unhealed let me sit with you and listen to you say what God cannot promise to give you.

TRASH

I searched through expensive restaurant trash bins in midtown Manhattan with a fourteen-year-old creaseless face, needle tracks rushing down both arms, hunched in what I pretended was no more than a treasure hunt with Angels grieving on watch. I held on like a hostage to each day like it was my last in life, roaming the streets like a character in a Dickens novel and after getting high with the stars gliding over me on the abandoned building rooftop called home with God absolving nothing. I imagined being with my two siblings, going to school, having countless adventures reading books and listening to mother stammer her Rosary after drinking too much ale. when I visit the city that kept me breathing, recall the ways it led me to fall into grace or when I walk by the spots dreams squatted with me the broken history of my family and people rush me. I stopped wondering how long these things will live, when they will fade away and decided to live by staying close to those who suffer in the world.

LAST NIGHT

last night with the persistent
chanting of cicadas producing
wordless hymns, I gazed with
you upon the moon showing
our love. your hair blown like
the leaves at midnight danced
like on the windy hills walked
in a foreign land. your voice
tumbled into me and each beautiful
word leaving your throat directly
for my quivering soul made their
way to our place of peace, plenty
and innocent love. with you the
shadows have lost their way and
in this flawed world I will forever
flee to the places filled with your
graceful kindness and touched by
your slender dark hands.

STREET VENDOR

they don't want to know the
tricky life you live pitching
tamales from a street cart on
the corner. they have never
imagined life feeding your kids
only once a day, keeping aside a
little spare change to buy your
children's notebooks, hiding from
hundreds of eyes mercilessly after
you and what it is like to wake on
days in the city when it rains. you
stand all day on the corner with the
scent sometimes of churros seducing
you with memories, the street growing
busier by the hour, the chatter of Spanish
carrying you past the American boulevard
to the village streets you played and that
still keep childhood secrets. you arrived
at the corner one dark morning barely
awake with young street walkers around
laughing on their way to rest and the old
Jewish man who lives in your building was
the first stranger to say buenos días like he
knew about long journeys.

HARLEM HOSPITAL

in 1969, I was sitting at a window in
Harlem Hospital in a heroin detox program,
with fourteen-year-old eyes wide open for
the first time in two years, tired like a New
York City pigeon on a fire escape, beside me
The Lord of the Rings trilogy, becoming aware
life itself is a high and a little closer to death
thinking about the home that kicked me out
to the streets. I spent each afternoon at that
window refusing to give up hope for all the
kids on the block who were strung out, thrown
away or locked up. I recalled all the sad songs
the Puerto Rican alley cats harmonized in a hall
of Papo's building before one-by-one the ground
swallowed them up, the hundreds of times I felt
nailed to a tree by American sin and the foolish
thought of keeping watch for the day the dead
would rise. Yeats would say I wanted heaven's
embroidered cloth so full of light but settled for
poor Spanglish boy dreams. I walked by Harlem
Hospital last week, recalling the many times I just
about died, letting Lenox Avenue see me cry, giving
thanks that hope never did expire and still declaring
the strength in a little faith. but you would call me a
liar if ever I said death in the barrio has no sting and
never leaves one bruised and weeping!

APRIL 7, 1985

I have written many words
in the years that followed
your death and mourning
picked me for a friend. the
secrets of life hardly started
when you left the world so
prematurely suited up for
the ground after my morgue
visit. we chased friends up
the side of mango trees, swam
in public pools for whites only,
broke night on streets listening
to salsa, and cried when Joey
died of an OD on a Fox Street
rooftop. I remember the Easter
Sunday when you said goodbye
and how we talked about living like
kids for the first time with Tia
in Kingston, Jamaica. child of God
the earth goes on, yet dear brother
four decades after your funeral, I
still dress in black waiting for time
to heal the wound.

STUPIDITY

when you enter
the quiet day
hearing
the news at first light of
the fascist trumpeters'
of stupidity
set
your mind
to
thinking
what is America.
you may say
with the
martyred theologian
there is
no defense
of
stupid
save piles
of poppycock
pressed
into ignorance for
the barbarous masses
who strut
victoriously
and end sipping
coffee
with a devil

in American gardens.
when all is said,
wake
to the pale colors
of morning,
a language
that will not
kill
and
the cost of
knowledge
that
helps you
narrowly escape
the
unprecedented
idiocy of the
right wing
    tossing
        shit.

THE PHILOSOPHER

the professor who came to class
wearing a Greek fisherman's hat
who found himself in the shadows
playing in Plato's cave addressed
his students rejecting the orthodoxies
keeping them from a view of the outside
world. he had a fondness for talking of
dim reflections in a mirror, poorly cast
shadows on the back wall of life and the
problem of freedom for chained prisoners
never close to it. like Euripides in Ohio,
he spoke with the modes of thought and
feeling of his generation to youthful listeners
unabsorbed by the riddles of being and the
apparent violence the world needs. the aging
professor was an observer of others who in
his classroom took students by the hand and
with threadbare words startled them to name
what is ordained to everlasting life. like Job,
he read Plato's dialogues slowly to his students
and then would pause to accuse God in heaven
of injustice and the boundless failures of love in
us all. I recall no one entirely agreed with the
philosopher's ideas and they smiled when at the
end of a class the old professor admitted not to
understand the world any better, yet they eagerly
paid attention to his generous allowance of
thought helping them soar for a few moments
on earth.

STREET FAIR

in my lower east side with
its mural walls exactly painted
with a complicated seeing eye,
a group of boys formed a quartet
to sing on the slanted sidewalk of
second avenue. one of the songs
shared with the brilliant laughter
speckling the street fair was the names
of kids painted on a wall of a building
on Avenue D dripping in its own way
with prayer. the pedestrians strolled in
their fondest dreams, an elderly Jewish
man munched on a hamantaschen
with smiling eyes disclosing his years of
longing, tired priests, teachers, workers,
undocumented maids, winos, mothers,
fathers, widows, Puerto Rican boys and
girls, and many others walked the Avenue
on this beautiful God blessed day and no
one deafened to strangers. not a single pair
of eyes looked straight on the Avenue this
day and the hundreds of tongues speaking
different languages were in motion like they
were on pilgrimage on the Jordan trail to
Petra. once you stepped into the street the
wondrous human river pulled you onward
to places of laughter and play, and I suppose
that is why I folded a piece of the day into
my pocket and still carry it with me.

AMERICAN DREAM

the ones who brought their children
north, harvesting the fields, working
the restaurants, washing dishes, cleaning
floors, tending lawns, planting gardens,
stocking shelves, taking care of little white
children and sometimes changing their
Spanish names are the beautiful ones who
call this country home. the ones in search
of welcome, who walked many miles on
borderless earth to get here, who crossed
the river into Texas like it was the Jordan,
who inherit the aging tenements, inferior
schools, abandoned churches, and detention
still believe shadows keep them safe. the ones
who stumble with a new language, with ears
filled with the sounds of rejection, who cry
each day for their American born children
rejected in the land of the free, the ones made
objects of liars, the women who escaped rape,
torture and femicide are the ones who know
hope has wings. the ones who gathered like
migratory birds to make the crossing, who
came expecting to find God's country are new
Americans from different places who help the
nation stay in its dream.

LOVE SONG

I sit here this early morning before the light imagining the love song not yet written for you, the mountains, rivers and oceans eager to meet you, the clocks refusing to report time, and all the beggars in the city on corners shouting your dear name. the words will come to me like first thoughts that can only belong to you, taking leave from the knots in my throat to live like before never existed. the Angels roaming the streets of heaven with their musical harps enchanting an eternity that does not change have never loved with the simplicity of a walk, in tenements where music plays, nor with the absorbing array of flowers in you. I will return in the morning with a lantern for the dark to wait patiently for the dear words that come in letters familiar to the two languages in me taking turns to offer a song to enfold you with love.

THE GARDEN

I turned to visit a garden with colorful flowers on a lot once the place of an old immigrant tenement in lower Manhattan. it is an unexpected reserve with multicolored petals widening the scope of the block with a fragrance that clings to dreams hatched on other shores. the sky was blue over the plot of flora, mothers holding children by the hand strolled past and no one was forbidden from entering. it is a place often visited by those labeled illegal in other parts of town to write letters about rivers swum, deserts crossed and new homes found. I adore watching children kick up dust chasing birds among the flowers, the old widows reading bibles, lovers kissing and friends who cherish each other. I love to breathe in this remarkably quiet place, to imagine the world a single color and listen to words jumping from the tongues of those who come for whatever reason to abandon sadness.

CRUCIFIED

the sight of an innocent man
nailed to a tree, the weeping
of a mother on ground beneath
him, Angels nowhere to be seen,
followers filled with things they
will not say, alone on the barren
wood of a lynching tree, death in
the morning air in place of peace,
love bearing the white criminal
whims known by slaves, people who
long to be free, the faces of lynchers
glad in their work and finally a ghastly
execution that makes us weep. the
last day of an innocent dark-skinned
human being's life, the Crucified God
seen in the flesh of my people that die
each day too soon, the mourners I hold
at the cemeteries of the poor, God looking
down in the comforting Black night and
the thousands of prayers from the inner
city barrios and slums we woefully say
for brothers, sisters, mothers, fathers, and
friends who will never see the sun. sweet,
Lord, are you listening? sweet Lord, how
long?

REVERSE BIBLE

there are murderers of truth
attending worship today who
read scripture backyards, turn
away from the message of the
man who cannot lie and insult
the poor whenever they find a
little bit of time to pray. it is
no surprise to me whenever I
hear these people speak how
fragile is belief in the God of
life who made ageless prophets
rage. the favors these hearts full
of hate seek never surprise me
by the ways they make sure the
twisted Cross stands straight
to burn with terror and keep the
meek of the created earth from seeing
the stone rolled away. the compliant
preachers agree with the thousands
of ways God is ridiculed by these
people craving English only for the
Bible, handshakes with the Devil
and guns to defend their kingdom
of nauseating feculence.

MORNING

one first day of Spring in
a New York neighborhood
the sidewalks were scribbled
with chalk, some girls jumped
double-Dutch, a few boys played
handball against the building and
the wrinkled faces of the Jewish
couple on beach chairs smiled with
the playful Puerto Rican children
forgetting evil. the day was exquisite
and not a single person then on the
block felt like Eve ejected from the
garden. this was the morning to be
told dreams matter and like bread on
a plate it filled empty stomachs.

DETOX

for more than one hundred years Harlem
Hospital has been on the Upper East Side
for lost junkies though the white folks downtown
never did know it. for many years it was the
place in the city that trained Black doctors and
nurses, when Dr. King was stabbed in the chest
on a visit to Harlem the procedure developed by
the master Black heart surgeon Dr. Maynard was
used to save the Reverend's life. my life made its
way to the hospital at the age of fifteen, they did
not expect a Puerto Rican boy carrying Tolkien's
trilogy to step into the ward to leave behind a dope
selling world that took up residence in his veins. I
remember being stripped, fumigated by an orderly
and feeling unprepared for the fear that visited me
in the English-speaking place, including looks that
questioned what a child was doing in a detox ward.
I recall the junkies on the floor were grown men with
too little belief that ten days kicking would at last set
them free. the words they shared with me trembled with
illness from one end of the ward to the other and their
eyes were always filled with tenacious sorrow. I recall
never once seeing Christians visit us to engage in bright
theological conversation about a God who saves but
I spent hours talking with young Black men dressed
with bow ties from the Nation of Islam that kept it plain
saying don't be a heroin slave. I was schooled for nearly
two weeks in that building on Lenox Avenue, hit the streets

clean then made my way back to the streets busy writing
their own psalms of lament that I had never once
heard or read. shit, I thought with a needle in my arm
and alone again on a South Bronx rooftop where do I
go from here?

THROWAWAY KID

I was several blocks away taking
long breaths in an abandoned building
curious about far off sounds I imagined
coming from home. in another world it
would have made little difference though
in this one I was just a throwaway Puerto
Rican boy. I got better by the day going
a long way on an empty stomach, too little
sleep and arguing with no one in particular
that poverty takes kids from their mothers
in America. some nights there were things
I only said in Spanish and on others I laughed
thinking about television shows that convinced
my childish mind the best way to become an
American was to eat apple pie. I recall a time
on a rooftop with a silvery moon and stars
above my head questioning the idea that God
made them and concluded the forgetful potter
way up in heaven never bothered to put finishing
touches on me. on my loneliest and fearful
nights, I tearfully remembered the beautiful songs
my mother sang and I prayed for her to come one
more time to cradle my head. though only twelve
the dead from the neighborhood were living inside
of me and I knew the English language could not
precisely say how I longed for the ordinary days
of being in a place called home. after all these years,
it is the vacant silence left from life as a throwaway

kid that haunts me and keeps me looking for the fluttering wings of Angels.

END-TIME

after the end of the world
there will be no guns, the
past will talk in tongues,
bitterness will be drunk
for eternity in big gulps,
we will question why life
unfolded in the hypnotic
thoughts of people full of
hate and every slaughtered
child will denounce us for
doing too little or nothing to
stop the taking of the lives of
the innocent who disappeared
in plain sight for ages.

PATRIOT FRONT MARCH

they marched the highly traveled road
duty bound to a white creed paraded
in front of the museums of freedom
recalling lives pitted against each other
in every name excluding difference and
dynamiting America with shame. with
covered faces these fanboys and girls of
white supremacy strolled the streets of the
nation's capital chanting delusions of white
superiority and pretending to finally disrupt
the colored world God made and they think
injures them. pity, they cannot see the human
beings they despise are wrapped with love
and godly dreams.

INSURRECTION

most of us think of January 6th
as three kings' day, or Epiphany
Day, but henceforth for citizens
in the United States it will be recalled
insurrection day, on which a legitimate
election got in the way, a time when
trickle-down idiots of a fired criminal
president refused allegiance, the election
certification period when lies, shame, hate,
blood, and death lifted lost cause flags on
the Capitol steps, ran them in the halls
of Congress along with acts of smearing
shit. who imagined the marble capitol
overrun by white nationalists and angry
hordes willing to scale walls, break
doors, batter the police and if possible
murder elected officials or hang Mike
Pence? who foresaw the conspiracy of
MAGA capped men, elected officials,
and security details acting in the name
of the portly loser who said fuck the
constitution, the rule of law and the
country, too? today, the whiny election
loser who slithered away to Florida is
still busy setting the house aflame and
the world is not short of believers who
think it is not enough to see this imbecile
pay the high price for betrayal of the rule
of law.

THE RIDE

I see someone moving at the
other end of the subway car, a
man leaning on the conductor's
door wearing a gold necklace
from which hangs the red, white
and blue of a Puerto Rican flag
keeping his eyes wide open for
the ride to a place in the Bronx
far from white hate. bendito, I
could almost feel the warm rain
falling on the island, hear school
girls gossip about the murmur
of the ocean, see them taking a
hand to walk out to sea and say
the names of natives enslaved
and ancestors who journeyed in
chains. our eyes meet just before
lights briefly go out and I want to
tell him soy Puertorriqueño-Jibaro
Guatemalteco-indio and I speak
Spanglish y otras cosas. the train came
out of the tunnel into a bright day
before stopping at Freeman Street
where the Nuyorican me ate bread
from the Valencia Bakery that tasted
right.

BARRIO

walls have messages,
infants weep, the kids
speak Spanglish, mothers
dream and worlds look
away.

EL PASO

I saw the men and women from
the countryside of the smallest
country south of the border who
are Brown in many shades and
never thought of themselves as
Hispanic. they said the term
invented in the United States
separated people with different
languages, cultures, suffering and
color of skin. I followed them on
El Paso streets relearning what it is
like to be afraid, to weep when no
one is looking, to talk about bitter
memories and mourn. I confessed
in a little café sitting with the new
arrivals that I was born dead in a
Northern city that called me spic,
the census Hispanic, my mother a
Boricua, my sister Latinx and the
White family that picked me up
when I was near dead living on the
street by their English names. I spoke
about a few stories known to me of
my displaced father and mother to El
Norte who fought for the weak, prayed
and passed away poorer than the day
they came. then, I confessed to them
in my beloved Spanglish that America

despite my fancy college degrees is a
strange home and people in my barrio
never confuse Hispanic with care for
the American dream.

MEDITATION

I want my hands to be like those of the lynched carpenter making appearances faithfully on earth. I want to capture history today to squeeze out darkness and proud white scorn until we admit God is undocumented. I want to burn all the maps with outlined borders, scorch calendars marked with incurable hate and feel divine rain going down us until we resume the walk to lost Eden. I want to feel the freshness of heavenly love, hear every breath of this living earth and confess God realizes ashes do not ever lay us to rest.

PARK BENCH

I lived on a park bench
dreaming a country away
from the fancy high rises on
Central Park West wrapped
in the *New York Times* and
cardboard boxes to fight off
the cold. when I trembled
alone strutting pigeons and
sparrows tumbling in the air
kept me company as the world
turned without pause and I sat
motionless waiting for a familiar
face to call my name. every now
and then the elderly out for a walk
would sit at one end with a smile
and I believed for a split second
in a flawless God. I tugged my belt a
little tighter each week to keep up
jeans familiar with the homeless and
hungry whom in my teen years living
on the streets I called people impatient
with hope. sometimes, when in a park
where leaves drift in the air I think of
the old bench like tourists to New York
I imagine think of souvenirs too many
years later.

THE CROSSING

what happened in the early summer
heat when I got kicked out of the tiny
apartment, went missing on the street
and yearned for an anxious family to
come looking for me? I wrote my first
letter to my mother in the Spanish she
left me to love, carried it to the library
folded in the pocket of the only pair of
trousers that came with me, strolled the
aisles in search of books telling stories
about people in the slums, bent corners
on the pages of a few of them, felt from
time to time the weight of a 12-year-old's
questions and kept in my hand a cross
given to me by Joey's mother in a santero
meeting at a Botanica on Fox Street. what
happened on the rooftops where junkies
gathered passing needles containing the
treasures of death, where American dreaming
never called my name and not a single kid
believed streets are paved with gold and
dollars are swept into mounds left in front
of the Perez bodega for the needy? well, I
learned a second language I use to make daily
border crossings in a country I call home
that calls me spic!

THE VALLEY

the chapel with carved wood
saints no civil war soldier dared
enter is across the street from
an old Ceiba tree where people
from the village gather with
weeping Pipil women to pray
and hear stories passed for more
than a thousand years. I visited
that chapel with flowers found
clinging to an altar with the scent
of Spring in them. grandmothers
dusted saints, a carved head of
Jesus and the Sacred Mother of
Peace who greeted visitors with
precious love. I visited early in
the morning to heal my soul with
faith that did not doubt a God who
sings in a tongue priests translate to
Spanish.

THE HAMMOCK

I think first of the time on
a hot afternoon we laid in
hammocks, the neighbor
across the alley screaming at
her son chasing a little sister
with a spider who was wailing
loud enough to wake entombed
archbishops at the cathedral in
the city center, dogs barking and
a rooster crowing on the porch of
the near deaf old man who played
first violin and founded the tiny
nation's first sinfonica. we talked
for hours about a civil war, the fight
among the poor held prisoners by the
rich, the postcard villages men fled,
women and children searching for a
different life in a Northern country
hating Indians and the once enslaved.
you very innocently asked what is the
biggest animal in the world and I tried to
recollect articles from National Geographic
to tackle the topic. we took turns proposing
God's creatures and ended passing time
fascinated by our raggedy imaginations.
when it got quiet, I chuckled about my time
with this old man defined by the clarity of
love and simple thoughts holding things in

place in a nation wanting more than heaven
to put an end to years of earthly butchery.

EAST HARLEM

a woman sings in the subway
station with watering eyes and
the word downtown is behind
her with an arrow pointing to steps.
signs are posted in the station saying
passengers are not allowed by law to
cross the tracks, litter, or spit though
nothing prohibits singing. a crowd has
gathered to listen, young and graying,
dark and pale, and speaking more languages
than the song smiles in the open air. on the
platform, riders could read an excerpt from
Keats' "To Autumn" thanks to the genius of
subway management, then a fragment of Whitman,
and Emily's lyricism in large print. after listening,
I headed to the uptown side of the tracks to catch the
train to Spanish Harlem, make my way to 104th and
Lexington Avenue to have a long look at a mural painted
by James De La Vega of my dear friend the late Puerto
Rican poet Pedro Pietri. you know, we called him by the
name he loved, the Reverend, and his work is poetry in
motion even when not hanging on subways. I thank Pedro
from time to time and the days we spent dodging, ducking,
and rolling out of make-believe living rooms for the sake
of jibaro dreams.

LONG ISLAND

he came from San Vicente
to New York fresh with images
of women braiding each other's
hair in a civil conflict where life
and death were prepared by the
wealthy with a liking for cold war
guns. he travelled a long way to
the deportation country, hiding from
soldiers and passing burned down
churches with Christ slumped on a
cross in the ashes left by the fires set
by uniformed killers. he found work
in Nassau County in a Home Depot
parking lot where his first English words
were, "pick me." days never end without
him giving thanks to the God of gossip
who in Spanish talks softly into his ear
to keep him a step ahead of workplace
raids and harm from gangs roaming the
formerly white Long Island streets. he
wires money each month to his sister for
the care of her kids and he stopped visiting
God in stained-glass-window churches that
have forgotten the wounds on the colored
man nailed to a tree.

THE MASSACRE

I can hear the pitch of your
voice reaching us from the
silent shallow grave in which
soldiers left you, when light
grows dim at dusk I can nearly
hear the things you left unsaid
to those men dressed in green
fatigues with rifles that never
considered the truth when they
faithlessly buried you with cold
war conviction. I sat many times
with the Belgian priest to make a
long list of every crime no longer
remembered by those in America
who paid for the bloody civil war
in the name of a God who delighted
in the betrayal of the poor. I will
never stop mourning for you, the
children slaughtered, the mothers
raped and burned, the priests and
pastors disappeared, abuelas with
slain smiles and the innocent after
all these years who have turned to
dust on ground that is spread now
in green. I have only a few words
for God who did not listen to the
stones crying about the innocent
dead who never stop testifying and

their contemptuous executioners full
of life, and free. God, make them pay
for their crimes against the slain.

DEADLY SINS

they talked about deadly sins
finding us out, knocking one
night on the apartment door,
showing up in the middle of
a stick ball game on the block
cursing Spanglish and plotting
to take us down. Julio told me
they would fly around like Poe's
Raven marking us for horror on
the corner, peeling away every
sign of faith that walked out of
the Catholic Church with us to
deliver us to evil. If only the
European migrant priest knew
something about his flock on this
piece of earth with so much dying,
he would have changed his brand
of pious gibberish, and realized not
one Puerto Rican kid had fallen far
from grace. kids around here try to
suck up life from the bodega, school
and church while questioning the
stupidity of biblical labels keeping
many blind to suffering human beings
spat on by shameless braggarts.

TOWN HALL

the town hall meeting, treated
to a news platform catering to
a racist and hush-money-paying sex
criminal, has approval by executives
voluptuous with hypocrisy and
ignorant of the tragic face of the
systemic betrayal of equality, freedom,
and democracy. the man
just found guilty of sexual battery
who has never shown signs of God
within him or listened to the sounds
of a lamenting world and toiling land
for his treachery is delivering more
lies. the final hollering will be heard
from sea to shining sea about how a
cable news network demented by capital
and ratings climbed in bed with a man
who will not rest until America is devoured
and imbeciles that look the other way are
consumed by their bullshit and political
deceptions.

DELICATE

you spent the fragile years here
living in the building next to the
little park with the trees that are
speechless though never lifeless
down here. your world has been
studied with magnifying glasses for
years held by hands accustomed to
resting on desks in affluent universities
not accepting dark girls with halting
English from countries getting USA
aid and packaged to live in star-spangled
banner craze. you know the world of
poets, novelists, artists, and philosophers
never heard by people with too little time
to study what others think on the Southern
side of the border or even know about love,
hope and sorrow. your days were numbered
before birth, ended too soon and they still
speak little of you in ivy league schools and
churches that forget to fear the Word dropped
from heaven to make crooked ways straight.

COLLECT POND PARK

the Georgia girl came to arraignment
day in New York City screaming for
the insurrectionist charged with over
two dozen felonies and letting the big
world see her tedious insanity. beside
her stood Santos the serial liar and yarn
spinner despised in Queens to complete
their sickening journey unable to do harm.
from the Collect Pond Park with daffodils
in bloom the sculpture of Medusa holding
Perseus's head in one hand and a sword in
the other made by the Argentine-Italian artist
Luciano Garbati cast its morning shadow
reversing the old narrative of delight taken
from the lifeless body of women. the irony
of the art depicting victims of abuse exacting
justice alone denounces the MAGA imbeciles
who fled the little park, while it stares down
the New York County Court House where a
disgraced man who boasted of grabbing women
by the genitals cannot play the idiot nor bully
in front of a Latino judge and Black prosecutor.
today, the disgraced former occupant of a house
built by slaves was the image of the criminal
always in him.

SEASONING

beans could not go better with
rice at the Formica table in the
one-bedroom apartment kitchen
with plastic covered furniture in
the living room. this dish college
kids called health food has given us
life like the Spanish floating from
the radio kitchen saying that tongue
is a keeper. the Irish kids in the same
building who would come over to eat
learned to love rice and beans along
with rolling their Rs with the sofrito
inhabitants moving into the tenements
abandoned by other white folks on the
block. we sat at the kitchen table at least
a couple of nights a week never foreigners,
poor together in wealthy New York, always
Catholic in different parts of the church and
filled by the same Holy Ghost under the South
Bronx sky.

FATHER

your ashes were spread across
the ocean shore and become more
familiar to me than shattered family
life I keep in a pocket of forgetting.
your absence was more conversant
than starlight, and when you father
were around in vastly noisy evenings
horror fell into our souls when you
pounded mother into bloody tears and
a puddle of sadness. we went to Mass
with the young woman you beat, heard
there is a place for missing fathers the
great potter has made, and wept about the
way darkness in your life of Guatemalan
exile unraveled on us. I am writing to you
after talking with my youngest son who said
Dad we are Christians and we forgive. you
left this world years ago and elderly years
did not keep you from cruel indifference. I will
say thank you for filling me with Spanish, giving
me a little of your indigenous ways and wherever
you are forgive my trespasses like I do forgive
you.

THE ROAD

I left the barrio hundreds of
times growing up though was
not reported a runaway to cops
or priests. my exit always came
with a daily junkie ritual started
at age 12 that involved cooking
dope in a bottle cap, drawing it
into an eyedropper with a needle
at its end and putting it in a good
vein on the arm used these days
for writing. I left the block by the
nod, lived the seconds in spaces
owned by a rush, was more than a
few times slapped back to life by
strung out old men and learned to
be a special needs kid. daily, I left
the streets high, lived waiting between
injections, never saw the inside of a
church, a public school, a furnished
apartment, my mother's flattening
nightmares or the nearest exit from
being sick. when my feet finally hit
the ground, I ran out of junkie time,
volunteered at a suicide hotline for
lost kids in a Spanish Harlem project
building, refused becoming a coroners
next friend, listened to words full of
gravity and started walking the road

not taken past the buildings where
junkies scream and the people who
do not earn much lay awake nights
wondering what it means to be made
in the image of God.

DARLING

we are nearer to God in
this common place full of
dreams and wakefulness,
darling. here you remain
closer than the laughter of
kids playing hop scotch on
the sidewalk, brighter than
the light of day and more
familiar than prayer. I have
not been happier with the time
aging us than inventing life
together on this ancient earth
and seeing wrecked villages in
Spanish-speaking valleys come
back to life. when final sleep calls
me to eternal rest it will not keep
me from singing you.

WOMAN

you have watched the moon drift
across the sky for more than seventy
years, imagined it playing tag with
clouds, looking over your shoulder
while you moved forward each day,
even occasionally thinking it staring
down from the heavens with a big old
smile. you have never stopped acting
like a little girl curious in the woods,
the schoolyard, the back pew of church
and the places where you found thousands
of ways to scream with utter delight in the
idea of a world without end. you talk of
yesterday recalling voices and stories that
have more life than the nights God has
made like the one about the Belgian priest
who travelled after seminary across the great
pond to move across decades with people
battered by a civil war. I love to sit with you
into the late evening emptying silence with
the peace that disrupts melancholy and lets
light come in.

RESTLESS

the restless waiting is getting
to me like thirst when walking
in the desert. I am alert each
day to the possibility of divine
whispering in my ear but meet
silence. no matter how many of
us begin the day with prayer and
singing in the storefront that was
once a barbershop heaven comes
up short and even Moses's tablets
tossed down the tenement's steps
would prove unconvincing of any
cosmic truth. I am afraid the local
parish has carried us with promises
no closer to divinity despite the very
careful reading people on the block
have given to the book of stories and
the Word made flesh. I have been going
up the ladder rung after rung, to a place
oxygen-scarce, where faith is a little
more crippled and the ancient voice
still says nothing. today, I will pause
again on the tenement steps to listen
and refuse the terrifying thought that
groundless being speaks louder than
God.

JUNKIE BOY

Angel was the first to push a
needle into his skinny arm on
a roof top while his father who
was a mailman was delivering
SSI and welfare checks. each
fix produced a rapture beyond
the Pentecostal storefront on
the corner once a synagogue
that flickered hope on a block
twisted by a plague striking kids
like lightening. when he was
done you could hear feet in
an old pair of dingy white high
top Converse sneakers slapping down
the building steps ready to catch
the latest news about little Victor
preparing to ship out to Viet Nam,
Joseph mugging the white kids
from Connecticut who rolled into
the Bronx with brand new cars to
buy dope and Bobby beaten by the
cops serving negligence and abuse
like priests offering communion in the
church. one fine summer night, at the
age of fifteen, Angel OD'd and the
word went out from the basement to
the rock out at sea and everyone was
speechless save his crying father

who prayed and listened to an
immigrant priest recite words for
one more life his Lord did not
save.

REVELATION

heaven is stooping toward the
street this morning inviting us
to patience, to dare confess the
inadequacy of questions about
the meaning of life or the man who
bleeds to death on wood and nails
some say for all. this morning is
unlocking to the sound of birds,
distant barks from a dog eager to
roam and God mumbling, again.
ancient winds will polish the old
sidewalks to prepare them for people
midway-to-nowhere, smiles will appear
on pedestrian faces who see an elderly
lady catching a child with a backpack
too big leaping into her arms and then
it will be impossible not to see the land
of milk and honey clearer than a sermon
about God disclosed in things.

SHORT

the old woman told me life is
short for the precious seconds
offered, too delicious no matter
how long the string of foolish
decisions, often terror for the
innocent and grasped sometimes
in the gracious splendor sold in
church. she said life is too short
for the world that breaks you and
to remember the divine promises
that make one burst into song. a
chilly wind followed a crosstown
bus breathing heavily from East to
West and I thought this old woman
full of light is keeping the darkness
completely away.

COLOSSAL SILENCE

no one on this block carried a Swiss
army knife packed with tools for on
these streets it was useless. here kids I
know carry survivalist blades, some of
them named for dead brothers, and more
than a few stuck in Brown skin and long
forgotten. the traces of fighting can be
seen at the edges of the sidewalk, the old
sneakers tossed over the telephone wires
worn once by Puerto Rican boys who are
recalled in church and rest today beyond
Promethean light. I remember a night, we
prayed for a visit from the Holy Spirit in
the hallway of Monica's building pleading
for knives not to have the last word by just
delivering us to early graves. for inexplicable
reasons the prayers we said in both languages
could not coax a word from heaven for we
were treated to the same colossal silence from
a God who apparently was fond of having the
poor take up church collections for heavenly
mansion repairs. when Wilfredo was stabbed
we even offered more intense prayers but nothing
changed!

CONGAS

they love to hear the congas played
on Saturday mornings with dancing
and prompt smiles on faces in naked
history. they listen to the drums until
their hearts are moved to lift the veils
covering the dreams in them. they have
carried salsa for generations in this city
pounding beats of struggle on stormy
days that are often too much for the
white violins treating a midtown crowd
to Mahler forgetful of his perfect clarity
of loss. there is an elderly woman with
a bag of groceries coming to the bench
with conga players and her face quickly
takes on a hue of ecstasy when stopping
to listen to the rhythm that reveals eternal
Spring. everyone hearing today is fully
convinced when the world ends pigeons
will wildly circle the buildings and brown
faced old men will be slapping drums to
signal the last sigh.

DREAM

morning arrived with church
bells ringing and a gentle rain
touching everyone. there was no
doubting a new day was peeling
away darkness and time tossed into
the world since the beginning fell
by the minute. I listened to footsteps
rushing to the subway station and
whispered beloved I dreamt last
night of birds chirping in the sickly
trees in the little park where the old
men play dominoes talking of never
ending affection, a more just world and
life for peace.

OLD WOMAN

a single flurry of snow tumbled
to earth finding rest on a florid
hat worn by a homeless woman
who sings to tourists that roam
Broadway persistently lost in
the world. you can see in her
eyes the countless years life has
leaped to other places to sample
air the lady had never known. she
wrapped her body in gold curtain
cloth likely found on the upper east
side of town and trembled with the
city that always listens to her sweet
voice full of here and now, sadness.
the pandemic years are over, people
are seen on every corner talking and
this old woman who sings for her bread
staying scarcely a step ahead of the
dead will continue ringing bells for
others who will forget her.

SWEETHEART

you came to the door this evening
to laugh with me at the dictator who
cannot keep the moon from crossing
the sky nor lovers from carrying what
is beautiful in them. even if tyrants cut
out my tongue it would not have kept
this zealous love from touching your
body without a word. not once could
bitterness find me despite the trumpets
of civil war sounding on the graves that
made us weep. sweetheart, in the world
keeping us nameless, I declare your slender
hand in the darkness taught me the only way
to love is to make worldly suffering answer
to God.

BORROWED

I walked the Bronx streets today using my daughter's legs to carry me across the avenues, the alleys and into buildings. I complained about the cold morning though her legs did not tremble for they were busily moving around with their own dreams. they took me to Southern Boulevard, stopping in a little park to observe three wild cats eating bread left for them and made their way over to P.S. 20 where I recalled hearing in a school assembly a group of kids on congas tapping out music against the end of the world.

EASTER

come Sunday we will wear clothes
bought on Delancey Street from an
orthodox Jewish store specializing
in barrio rags for Easter. the kids
who worked shining shoes, carrying
old ladies' groceries for tips, mopping
tenement hallways for supers never
minded not reading a single story of
Jesus about him dressing up slick for
the public. come Sunday, we will go
to Mass for the second time in a year,
let go beautiful Spanglish chatter in
pews, admire the flowers with sweet
scent luring the Lord to the church, the
streets, the overcrowded tenements, and
the long list of names from South of the
Border packed in church. come Sunday,
we will fill our stomachs with God in
bread, stagger like corner drunks who
beg for alms, then like the holiest kids
head to the subway station for an Easter
ride to the other side of town to Central
Park to parade all these bargain street
threads.

THE PROJECTS

I have been haunted by the
police sirens rushing down
the street to the projects on
Avenue D that have messages
spray painted on bricks walls. I
am troubled by the way police
cars rush to the place called a
tombstone by the Puerto Rican
kids who like to hang in court
yards and are first to get kicked
by steel-toe shoes on flat-feet. I
look out the window for the ones
who are punched and slapped like
pizza dough, those who have so
many things in common with the
poor Jew born in the stench of a
stable, those protesting hate and
denouncing the Christians who went
out of their way to murder King and
Romero. I see Tito and Lefty headed
to the projects so I shout to them walk
toward Third Avenue where University
students roam about in white skin, and
unbothered.

THE RETURN

with the start of this day
rusty and flaking like an
old fire escape, seeing the
the old man with a soiled tee
shirt chain smoking on the
park bench, next to him a
conga player coughing, the
city sparrows skipping on the
sidewalks, I experience morning
dancing with your memories. the
spirits have come to me from the
Salvadoran mountains, floated for
thousands of miles, jumped over
the border Wall and offered me
the scent of Izote on the broken
stoop. by the time abuelas open
window blinds, I will declare my
love for you and that other country
torn by civil war I call by name and
known as home.

WOKE

woke on the bus just hours ago
when the Puerto Rican girls were
mocked by white boys calling them
spics and Muslim girls with covered
heads and necks were told to go back
to where they came from like they were
not born right here. woke long before
reaching my stop hearing words firing
out of mouths wanting to wipe history
of lynching trees, the sisters who saw
brothers disappear, the lands taken by
force, the voiceless people who were
auctioned, worked, beaten, stomped
and left disfigured. woke again just
minutes ago, thinking about slavers,
cops, judges, rapists, racists, imperialists,
and hearts widened by hate that spread
misery on earth. woke recalling terrified
kids in schools with shooters on the loose
and looking for clocks to chime mercy for
a world ignoring the costs of sin.

STRANGER

you have more to say than what is
written in books removed from the
public school libraries to silence the
history of wicked deeds in a world
awake with crucifixion and mindless
to sin. you have touched Brown flesh
to brush away desert dust, scribbled
your Spanish name in the sand, waited
on the Mexican side of the Wall in the
dark and imagined for the other side
the grammar of peace missing from
those living on their knees. you have
stories to tell, hefty crosses to haul and
protest sounds to make in the towns you
expect to enter. your mouth will denounce
ghastly inhumanity, condemn racial hate,
devour the white side of history, tear down
the doors blocking the truth that discloses
your wounds. you are significant in this
place cursing you and the tattoo cross
on your ankle will someday dance on the
graves of American racist brutes in the
name of the unfinished business of a just
God.

TIME FOR WOKE

ladies and gentlemen, fellow citizens, xenophobes, white supremacists, racists, malefactors from Mainstreet America, we the people are here to spend the rest of life loosening native tongues, hidden in plain sight, laboring to live, we are undyingly present, been here for hundreds of years before the country learned an English word, radiant in Black and Brown skin through day and night, and spend the long hard work days pitying the ignorant who refuse to see and embrace their own history. guardians of the lost cause, lovers of division, red-necked, and proud liberal white folks of the USA, those who want to hang us, burn us and toss us piece by piece across the border, get on your knees to thank us for the country we have made inch by inch while God spoke in the places we bled until we shouted from the highest peaks of your purple mountain majesty: hallelujah. people of the Mayflower, asleep on Plymouth Rock, generation after generation of liars, thieves, colonialists, money-grubbers, and blasphemous killers take the time you need to be schooled about the people you will never kill. hateful ladies and gentlemen, there is a path for you to take, ashes to follow made by the fires you set that will lead you to us waiting for you with the God who freed slaves.

BOOKS

I learned a few things roaming
the aisles of many bookstores like
where to find Borges, Anaya, Angelou,
Auden, Baldwin, Hughes, Whitman,
Marquez, Morrison, Allende, Williams,
and Neruda. their stories have haunted
me now beyond words, taught me to see
mystifying images in the world and use the
rumbles of language attempting to capture
the vast reality it names. I have managed the
years with them dizzily glancing at their pages,
enjoyed the huge mystery of the bookstores and
libraries where their work sits on shelves to be
touched. they prowled cities, villages and more
than a few countries with me talking with the
innocent and cruel about truths named by the
mythologies and religions birthed in a complex
world. I learned about enchantment from these
authors and the importance of returning to the
simple sentences of sadness and joy found in
the barrio each day.

COVENANT SCHOOL

how long can we go on saying prayers
for the ethically innocent victims of gun
violence? when will we stop pledging
allegiance to guns pretending to keep
children safe? here in America where
books are banned shooters enthusiastically
pull triggers in grocery stores, Walmarts,
movie houses, churches, Malls, drag queen
shows, or to kill teachers and innocent pupils
making public space from coast to coast a crime
scene. when will legislators, schools, police,
courts and clergy learn from the dead, the families
mourning them and friends who never stop weeping?
I cannot find words to say another prayer in a country
seeing kids killing kids, white men are killing Black
and Brown humanity and criminal politicians who are in
love with violence they have never experienced. I curse
the imbeciles who sacrifice children to their beloved
Moloch, the gun. today, six people were shot to death,
among them three nine-year-old students and the young
woman doing the killing had a handgun and two AR-style
weapons with her like the lapel pins worn by legislators
or observed in a family Christmas card. shit, tell me you
will stand beside the grave of the slain, tell me you will
not put up with more innocent lives lost, tell me you find
guilty the politicians against gun control, tell me you will
connect the dots to end the sickening season!

NAZARETH

they sat on the stoop that night
with slender necks adorned by
Rosaries that were blessed by an
Irish priest in Mass, questioning
the good that came out of Nazareth,
paying attention to abuelas on their
way to market and thinking about
spray painting one great message in
Spanglish. these kids taken to the big
church on Sunday had questions, after
Manny died of an overdose on a roof
hiding from the Military Police looking
for him for going AWOL to avoid being
sent to war. who cares to give praise to
God without asking about the fate of those
ruled for centuries with whips and chains?
the kids thought the people going to church
who spend wretched days begging for miracles
should be thanked by God for holding on to
their faith. the kids on the block think God
should also surprise Carmela with a miracle
to restore credibility in divine things. you see
barrio boys and girls reading troubled waters
want to know when the man from Nazareth
will come to put a stop to the white fists pounding
Black and Brown faces.

LISTEN

we wake up in a fresh new day
spending the hours imagining
where to find the clearest sight
of ourselves. we imagine language
that God walks with us though in
silence, flares up in our hearts at
the right moments and delivers us
in the best and worst of times to
the valley of life. the day is part
of a magnificent prayer just like
a multicolored flower pointing to
heaven without words, the amazing
silence inviting us to listen and the
wind whispering in our ear time to
let go. in the here and now of this
morning one only needs to make space
to get woke to the first and absolute
truth given in shared creation.

NO PASSPORT

the single mothers are sitting in
beach chairs bathed already with
sun screen to replace the umbrella
they do not own, tanning. they came
to America by plane, citizens like other
Boricuas, since 1917 having never even
seen a US passport, ready to find work
in factories, tagging coats on racks in
cheap garment warehouses in midtown
Manhattan, picking fruit in Florida or other
comestibles in some godforsaken state
that is under snow in long winters. they are
on the beach wearing the same smiles that
will be in their underpaid workplace, they
will never complain to the white boss, miss
a day of work or find a better day for rest like
this one at Orchard Beach. they have arrived
from a Caribbean Island that is an extension
of US empire, underclass citizens from the
shores of a Spanish- and sometimes English-
speaking colonial necropolis. they were never
undocumented yet know the meaning of having
to erase parts of themselves in a country writing
history without mention of them and absurdly
believing American means white. today these
women of every color stirring the Star-Spangled
Banner to new dreams are here for the long haul
no matter how many tomorrows the God of promises

has in store for a nation unkind to suspect mahogany citizens.

THE RIVERBANK

I have seen thousands of
suns rise on aching dreams
over the heads of people
with stories about a long
walk to a riverbank and
then across. the water
is cold, the night windy
and into this life they come
with bandages holding frail
hearts.

SAVIOR

Savior, take my hand on earth
where it really matters like Tito's
old man when crossing the street
and be divinity down here that looks
like Rosie who walks Simpson Street
on sale, the shoe shine men who came
North from down South and then stop in
the Aquacero Restaurant for a last supper with
the meek. Lord, stop wasting time in faraway
heaven that does not need you and make your
way down here to the block with empty bellies,
single mothers working more jobs than they
have time in a week, strung-out kids who no
longer praise and all the people that hurt
to breathe. Lord, knock on the apartment
door where Julia lives, go inside to see the
candles next to photos of her dead teen son,
another burning for your mother, then dare say
something to her about darkness and wickedness
in the world. Lord, let yourself be found walking
these streets right soon or the whole damn barrio
turn away and you will weep like you did long ago
in the city where you perished.

PEACE

we have craved peace long
before priests in church urged
us to pass it around to prove
it near. we have searched for it
longer than the grass has grown
in sidewalk cracks, like finding
sanity each morning before hard
work, or like telling each other
peace is what Spanglish prayers
bring. we have searched for the
kindness peace offers without any
cost to the homeless, the hungry,
the loathed, the ill, the poor and
victims of war. we have walked
the streets in silence, heard voices
streaming out of apartment windows,
greeted children raucously playing
and watched stray dogs with tails
shaking begging to slip into the fun,
and every hateful word that was ever
swallowed could not with judgement
change the faithfulness in our beautiful
welcoming souls.

MEMORY

my life has reached the place
called memory unfolded in the
most unexpected places like a
napkin placed in one's lap. they
carry me to the spots that keep
my eyes on the horizon of Puerto
Rican beaches, bathe my soul with
incense from hundreds of churches
at home and abroad and take me to
unexpected voyages in search of a
place where I belong. I am restless
steering each day in barrios with
people hungering for bread and
caught in the sickening clutches
of a world without love. they
cannot speak more clearly of the
desire for perfume sprinkled on
the sidewalks leading me with
past darkness to terrain granting
me the right to live.

STREET MARKET

the street carts with fruits and
leafy greens in cardboard boxes
from places used to bartering are
out in the early morning light, ripe
smells fill the air dancing it up with
the sounds of English, Spanish and
Cantonese and an irregular breeze
chills shoppers who anticipate real
bargains. there are bright signs on
Mulberry Street done in careful Chinese
calligraphy thrilling faces on the sidewalk,
the characters are not translated into
any familiar tongue that has grown older
with me but I feel a deep gladness to see
them on this street. one block over, at
the entrance to the subway, a Mexican
woman sells churros from a metal grocery
cart to people who cannot name the treat
despite hearing the name shouted twice.
language here finds its way to hand signs
after leaping distances with street vendors
who walked across deserts.

THE HEIGHTS

in the Heights bachata
plays on the sidewalk
alongside of rapid-fire
Spanish describing a day
showing up on the block with
one packed bag. gone is the time
of grand estates, waves of German
Jews, the Yeshiva University and the
Aufbau newspaper that reported Nazi
crimes and published Einstein and
Arendt. the Heights these days is
storefront awnings speaking Spanish,
chicharron people walking on the
sidewalks, kids jumping around on
St. Nicolas Avenue, colorful street carts
packed with exotic fruit and someone in
a delicious restaurant with a sweet voice
saying, ¿están listos? the Heights is life
without english labels and a place called
home by people fleeing tormenters, hungry
for bread and longing for the best side of
gorgeous humanity.

GRAVEYARD

I walked by a few cemeteries in
the city crowded with speechless
bones and the pure sounds of those
who visit to mourn. when I found a
seat on a quiet bench beside one of
them the coffins of too many friends
labored up river in my mind like an
endless line of skiffs with no one rowing
and headed to an unknown end. in silence,
I watched these wood boxes float along
questioning the permanent presence of
the divine in time, sure of the lives the
weathered gravestones spoke, doubting
church witnesses who talk of an eternal
place reserved for us and then more sure
one day I too would be floating up this river
not a single promise of time reaches. I
walked the grounds of the cemetery still
brilliantly dividing races, stopped to shed
tears for a murdered friend, placed flowers on
my brother's grave and stared at flattering
inscriptions on gravestones for so many
beloved and others prematurely taken away
from us.

CLANG

there is something in me that
never fully made its way to
a place of forgetfulness and
it arises oddly without any
warning. some nights I recite
sad lines about a mother who
was too young to offer love, an
Indian father wasted by hard work,
a brother the devil kept in chains
and life nearly drowned in a puddle
of sidewalk tears. I have spent hours
leaning into images of lost family,
inconsolably sifting memories like
feelings on cold nights in abandoned
buildings and forsaken mission houses
in Miami, Los Ángeles and San Juan. I
can almost hear the prayers said in
dope shooting galleries beside other
dreadfully lost souls and to this very
day experience the inescapable feeling
that something is missing.

RIO GRANDE

the river has many names
on the border turning here
and there for eyes to see,
with history too vast to ponder
and crossed by many since the
beginning of things. the river
has cuddled children, held the
swollen bellies of mothers
and promised to give a little
more life after being crossed.
the river is ancient between
two countries, a place children
are sometimes snatched from
their mother's arms by border
guards serving empire. the river
is a place clothes are wrapped
in plastic, tied with thin string and
carried like a sack of dreams to
another bank. the river is a place
to see brown faced border guards,
drowned migrant dreams and some
dashing across Texas in the palm
of God's hand.

JESUS

I saw you in the packed subway,
standing beneath a street light,
in a Ukrainian restaurant on 9th
Street, in the girls dancing to the
bachata pouring out of the Dominican
hair salon in the Heights, on the quiet
banks of the Hudson River, in the
menu at the Malecon, the coats on
Broadway pushed along by the wind
and in words leaping out of the mouth
of a storefront preacher. I saw you in
the scribbles on the building where old
men and women who cannot speak a
lick of English live, in the silence of
mute Lefty sitting on the stoop, on the
faces of the newborns smelling of milk,
the Puerto Rican mothers delighted to
smile and the kids baptized with the name
of a saint. I saw you touch the soft cheeks
of children who had come a long way, kiss
their skinny hands, exhale flowers and call
us all by name.

THE MARTYR

San Romero de las Americas you are murdered children, voiceless peasants, bloody valleys, mountains, rivers, villages, catechists, priests, pastors, women, and refugees. San Romero de las Americas you are a forgiving voice calling for peace, a Saint ignored by government, dismissed by America who the poor resurrect and sing. San Romero de las Americas you are the voice of an unknown God, the face of the poor, the hungry, the suffering, and a messenger of heaven for a divided earth. San Romero de las Americas you are the broken body of God, the blood of crucified people, the martyr of hope for the wretched of the earth. San Romero de las Americas no one in all the world will silence you, conceal your witness, or keep us from the future you declared more than once is not our own.

WEARY

tired at the end of the factory
day the living room with the plastic
covered sofa still looking new holds
a body. her eyes are closed and a
record player spins the latest Beatles
songs with her dreams rolling along
in 33 RPM. kids listen sitting on the
linoleum floor in the living room they
call a carpet, climbing the imaginary
music ship taking them for a ride to City
Island, across the dark water Sound and
out to sea without stumbling into border
check points. the Beatles-loving woman
back from the horrors of the assembly
line where she cuts zippers that others
sewed into garments is inhaling the music
in a cheap tenement living room with
copious cheer. she is in the habit of living
after work, of collecting memories from
the past to share with her kids, of kneeling
at the altar in her bedroom without doubting
God hears and always steadying herself to
be light in the tiny space called home for the
sake of her US born kids.

THE LABORERS

the morning fell on the streets
pausing to caress the faces of
hard workers speaking Spanish
with wounded tongues coming
out of hiding. they walked past
the church from which a band of
Angels never once came down to
comfort them or take home the most
tired. a couple of young boys who
quit school to work in a downtown
garment warehouse talked about not
leaving their bones in an overcrowded
cemetery before knowing something of
salvation. they were sugar cane cutters,
coffee pickers, potato gatherers, rusty
plough pushers existing for another day
in a bereaved city, people dreaming of
a journey on roads lined with flowers
and ending in better days. I joined them
heading to the subway station like a crowd
walking steadily on an iced lake in Central
Park amused by sunlight pointing out the
cracks to avoid.

PEACE

we have forgotten how to make
peace in a world that is dressed
for terror, driven by profits, sinking
deeper into darkness and unable to
touch the garment of God. we have
forgotten to let our mouths say the
word, to tremble at the harm done by
us, to weep about unlighted days, to
look upon the face of sorrow and
feel a part of it. not many recall
the blood of martyrs, the difference
between right and wrong, the dogged
equality of death, the lies that feed on
mortal souls and the truth that clearly
exists on earth. this word peace already
has so many speeches, has comforted the
weary, peddled kindness and begs today
like it will in weeks to come for another
hearing.

REMEMBER

I know the rooftops looking out
to the East River watched over
by stars, the boarded tenements
with old women on stoops, the
places where the widows go to
look up to heaven and the spots
you will always live better than
photographs. night after night,
I sit serenely above noisy streets,
roaming the memories of you, me
a little more wrinkled now that you
parted. tonight, I complain about
the shifting sand in hourglasses not
delivering us to places where darkness
is punched full of holes and death that
comes like a thief in the night cannot
find any of us.

MAUNDY THURSDAY

tonight, I remember Jesus said
wait with me at a table though
those words came from Angel's
little brother who shared the savior's
own name. no one on the block you
see doubted the word became flesh,
was arrested by official thugs, beaten
with clubs, abandoned by friends, pled
for mercy and the deliverance of love.
in the thinning days of faith, dressed up
with death and ceaseless weeping, the
barrio is closer to Christ than churches
putting off God's promises of life for
the bitter on earth. tonight, the holy
thing to see is Carmen Julia reduced by
men who buy her misery, the kids on
the block living in the nation of poverty,
mothers on the stoop with candles ablaze
with dimming light and the sweet faces
of abuelas cursing the world of Judas's
kiss. tonight, hope will need to wait for
another day!

THE PASSION

it is morning on Good Friday
the streets are not speaking and
churches are already filling with
murmurs headed toward the great
silence. we will spend the hours
before us searching the darkness,
trying to discern the meaning of
temptation hidden in the shadows,
questioning how a pallid cold body
nailed to a cross offers ultimate love
and redemption from beyond. it is a
good time to pray about events from
Gethsemane, to speak to the God
nailed to a lynching tree, to ponder the
Word made flesh that bled, and to weep
with the poor beneath the boots of those
who pledge allegiance to violence and death.
it is Good Friday and the world will again
relive God's death.

SIDEWALK

I am standing before a group of
cement masons pouring concrete
for a new sidewalk, watching kids
laugh like they were daring the next
sunset, a mother sticks her head out
of a window to shout for her boy and
the gang of workers look around
at the gathering crowd with dark
eyes widened by the dog barking
on Tarzan's fire escape. they have
labored for weeks around the city,
seen the crucified faces that crossed
borders, rivers, deserts, and even
toasted with a can of beer the dreams
of the bold broken English people.
when they finish I want to write the
names of abuelas with sketches of
their wrinkled faces in the cement,
leave whole sentences about the Brown-
faced elders who walked with rosaries
hanging on their necks to deliver kids
from bondage and thank the generations
who worked for pennies in the name of
days not made for dodging soldiers, gangs
and barbed wire lives. I will leave a note
in the hardening sidewalk about the workers,
too.

RISEN

across the Christian earth today
hallelujah is shouted for Christ
is risen by divine love in flesh
and voice for us. today, we sing
Christ in every living thing, the
One older than the sun, the urge
against all hate and the magnificent
kindness risen from the grave. keepers
of the word in books contentedly speak
today, the hollow ears from North
and South and East and West are
listening. now, we joyfully speak
Christ against wickedness has risen
and walks again on earth, to rest on
worn-out lips, to disentangle wounds,
keep us all awake to every hint of hope
and every sign of life now and beyond
the grave.

WAITING

in the great gathering of the
tired in tenements where the
living breathe thinking of other
lands and dust collecting dreams,
I let life come to me like the smell
of rain in Spring on the sidewalks.
we sat for hours on the stoop talking
about sweet things, weeping for the
wounds of others, chuckling about
the church adorned with flowers and
Miriam's child in a crib lifting her
head. I brought bread with me from
your favorite bakery ready for a river
tossing that helps us believe crumbs
floating to sea will reach that part of
the world laced with honey from God's
garden.

LANGUAGE CLASS

the language learners entered
the classroom making Spanish
noises that marched to the city
with them from another part of
looted earth. they are eager to
learn English and fearful about
speaking words too familiar with
putting life up for sale though they
would indulge the lessons to enjoy
wakeful hours at work and in the
tenements where you cannot burn
wood to cook meals. the strangers
in the room were ready to learn a
few sentences to carry with them to
work and to tiptoe around the city
with lines to hide their undocumented
status. I saw a lady kneeling one day
in front of her home altar, staring into
the eyes of a porcelain Saint and praying
in English beside a candle to God she
trusted understood.

PRAYER

prayer comes to the lips
of the voiceless to ask for
lost cause ruin. they come
in the darkness of night to
speak against the wicked
who stay up late to think about
how to cripple freedom for the
sake of white supremacy. let
the killing fields soaked with
the blood of those who suffer
in a society proud of its sadistic
criminality, racial persecution and
capitalist dictatorship find milk
and honey on the hills lined with
lynching trees. prayer comes to
those who kneel in the desert, in
stadiums against the bad cops, in
the houses of politics organized to
slaughter equality, through border
walls in defense of democracy and
reviled people in woke flesh with
heads thrown back ready for the
promised land.

LIAR

another worldly liar with
peddler's words, trinkets
and tedious charm with
odds unfavorable cannot
escape the ticking clocks
nor crows that will deny
him three times before the
legal bills are due. they say
the devil is a liar gargling
misleading words with his
corrupt tongue, never at
all guilty of sin, obscene
like the man who pisses in
the fountain of truth and is
the image of a life of lust
and rage. the big lie that set
the fabricator's pants ablaze
and made the nation weep is
now displayed for all to see
and it will not endure the law,
democracy nor truth to stage
more Klannish rallies. you
see light shines brightly on
criminal evidence and this
trust-fund loser has come
to this: the time to set things
straight in the name of truth
and accountability to the rule
of law.

NATIVE LAND

my native land is a street in
the South Bronx close to the
hospital where I was born,
never paraded by soldiers,
controlled by errant cops, a
long way from the border and
with a dividing line that runs
through it put there by white
downtown folks who invented
thousands of ways to keep us
down. in my native land, Black
and Brown children who are targets
of hate are not featured on nightly
news, talked about in the big white
churches or private schools. I can
tell you the days on the block slid
over me like a cross-town bus and
I saw many Black and Brown soldiers
home from rich men's wars roam the
streets in junkie skin mugging their
poor neighbors. I have kneeled in front
of apartment altars to pray to Saints about
a country that simply does not hesitate to
tell people like me you do not belong and
to say no matter the stony roads this county
tis of me.

NIGHT

everything behind the night
handed me slack questions about
the last church remaining in the
neighborhood with its experts
bringing messages that on the
block are centuries too late. no
one around these parts has had the
luxury to say the question in life is
to be or not, which is thought well
and good for the classroom with a
Shakespeare head on a bookshelf
and a map of the world with barrios
unmarked. I have only dusty answers
tonight, scrambled Spanglish from the
part of the city still speaking about the
synagogue that was on the corner next
to the barbershop that spoke Yiddish and
you can be certain old William would be
lost here like an Adam kicked the hell out
of paradise. the voiceless asked me to
denounce the crimes against the poor and
hateful creeds and I will not stop until the
world is right!

REALITY

my reality is known by
signs, once segregated
schools, white-only fountains,
and the poor. it is infinite
particles, imagined life, the
government deciding and
tortured thoughts. reality
is a single word, a blessed
search and the need to know
things change. reality is more
hope than imagined and a thing
they say just is.

PRAY TELL

it was hot the day we went to
the creek to swim with muskrats
floating on driftwood tossed
from the train bridge. Diamond
brought a big old bar of soap to
bathe in the unclean river since
the super turned off the water in
his building to save the landlord
money. we swam talking about
the bullshit classes in junior high
school that provided lessons good
enough to make every Puerto Rican
kid's eyes roll back. our mothers
dreamed of living in the Big Apple
and stretching out their arms to hold
people who did not speak Spanish like
them. we lived their broken dreams in
the city, got beaten by white cops, left
by churches on the streets to become full-
blooded junkies on the way to Golgotha
and made to feel like monstrous exiles in
the only place called home. so, pray tell
what comes next?

THE RADIO

the large face alarm clock
rang after a night of fidelity
in the Bronx to silence. the
morning news played in the
kitchen on a Spanish radio
station while a wrinkled hand
reached for American eggs
and cracked them and the
mother sang along to a tune
by Celia Cruz that reminded
the poor kids waiting to eat
they have music. Shorty knocked
on the apartment door for the
walk to school kicking Schaeffer
beer cans with friends he would
outlive, never forget and wonder
nights about the graves that kept
them. the morning on the block
was already busy with junkies
trafficking dope like they were
never church kids who ate Holy
bread in Saint John's Church. the
friends walked to public school
thinking about hanging signs on
the way with gossip about God
dodging broken English people.

GIRLFRIENDS

she was standing on the fire escape
calling down to the street to faces
walking south to the subway station
kicking up dust from rejected history
left on the sidewalk and looking for
signs of the messiah among them. the
boarded stores across the avenue were
unpacking for business and the fire escape
girl yelled to a friend she would be down
in ten minutes for the stroll to Simpson
Street with the blessed others who dared
hold on to dreams. the two girls walked
chatting about the place their mothers
left behind, the near empty church on
Hoe Avenue silent about what happens
on the block and Henry who became the
latest Spanish-speaking beggar to sit on
its steps raising money for wine research
and living on the kindness of others. they
spoke to each other tenderly about hope
in the world embraced by their migrant
mothers, stopped in front of a florist shop
to rest their eyes on a display of flowers
that offered a touch of salvation to their
dark bodies.

THE DAUGHTERS

in the building that warehouses
campesinos who once picked coffee
on mountainsides for pennies fatherless
girls have moved in each with a look in
her eyes full of probing when staring at
clouds above the city rooftops just to see
if fathers have changed into them to make
up for absence. some clouds were shaped
like folkloric giants entertaining daughters
looking up from the ground, others thinned
away until the girls could find no trace of them
and God who made things was left confessing
fault. the daughters from elsewhere do
spend time for better or worse looking for the
fathers with them too brief, they talk about it
on the way to school, stare down the streets for
as far as the eye can see and even light candles
in church, while glancing over their shoulders in
the event these men showed up in that house set
apart to take care of continuing needs. the girls
could not recall ever seeing fathers wave goodbye,
hearing them share stories about what they longed
to do in the world or what dreams they held for girls
like them. the girls who counted clouds together
held on to the thought that one day they might see
their fathers standing with flowers at the end of the
street.

THE BEGINNING

in the beginning there was the demand of gangs knocking on neighborhood doors collecting fees. in the beginning was the decision to leave that had been secretly forming in a mother's heart and in thoughts about not living with hunger, terror, suffering days and God knows what. in the beginning, hell set fire to the idea of heaven on earth and a mother looked for signs of God in the clouds, the desert, the river, the mountains, and the walk. sweet mother on the run with kids, I will pray for you to find a way until our deaf God hears!

SPRING PRAYER

on this quiet morning, I watch birds
bouncing on a grassy meadow pure
in each minute. it occurs to me to
thank heaven for keeping me in the
precious moment, allowing me the
simple joy of seeing darting creatures
of air, inhaling the pleasures of early
Spring managing to stand still and to
experience the world in ways leading
to the deepest confession that God is
love. the mysteries this morning burn
brighter than divine names offered like
torn bread for the hungriest who knock
on the doors of locked cathedrals. I have
never felt more saved or at peace with
the grace that permitted me these sweet
unearned passages of life.

THE WALK

I walked around the streets of
the city when others slept yelling
in the alleys, standing on corners
to weep about gone stores, movie
houses, eateries, old men playing
dominoes and the spectacle of kids
warming chilly days with games. I
paused to talk with convicts hanging
on stoops condemning with them the
houses, the offices, the families and
the churches overlooking their names.
I must tell you more than a few of us
mentioned the invisible border keeping
us caged, sentenced to a prison of shadows
and carried by hate to urban warehouse
graves. together, we have walked without
a visa from here to Jerusalem and collected
miracles on the way back with a few words
from a Holy language stuffed in bodega bags
for the church on Hoe Avenue and for use
the next team Joey ODs on the rooftop of
his mother's tenement.

NIGHT JOURNEY

walking in the night listening
to the tenements with God a
faint presence on the streets,
I heard singing inviting me
to see beneath the surface of
things. I saw flowers open
on a fire escape observing the
requirements of Spring and I
called upon the mystery in charge
of life. journeying alone that night
I was more aware time confidently
advances and is punctured by the
questions that march toward some
paradise whispering the precious
names of martyrs. walking to the
edge of the East River, I thought
hell dear Bertolt is not the city with
wilting trees and blushing people
heading nowhere with rash thoughts,
you see hell is history made by Herod's
thugs, murderers, and tyrants forcing
the innocent to flee.

SANCTUARY

consider the altar at the
church with the cracked
roof through which light
breaks in, where people
with open wounds recite
prayers to save themselves.
think with me about the
poor with bread on their
tongues unlearning the
world that eats them. imagine
for a moment the perfection
described in cloistered halls
disliked by tyrants who scorn
justice, demand obedience and
with manuals of vulgarity they believe
God hates. think about the divinity
that cannot be kept imprisoned on
on earth and speaks loudly with the
voices of the harmed.

THE MOVIES

I caught a movie on the big screen
with new stars rising to charm us
for a couple of hours. the children
sitting next to me giggled when the
heroine kissed the unlikely guardian
of the Universe who amassed good
deeds for the powerless while tossing
short glances of love to the alien girl
in his heart. everything in the fantasy
flick was irrational, occasionally brutal,
and saddled with the memories of an
audience's finest imaginings. the movie
crowd was entertained by the moral
consciousness of a plot unfolding the
struggle of good against evil and the
crowd roared whenever the villains got
their comings. we were all delighted to
see the misfit heroes saving the cosmos
along with one of their own and every
being worthy of a ride on a space-age
Noah's Ark. there were even moments
for Kleenex for the sentimental who were
blowing their noses when oneiric images
carried viewers to places for which no one
bought a ticket—nothing like the movies!

GENESIS

it is interesting God made
the people to spread like gossip,
dropping a few words to make
heaven, the earth, and things
that breathe. you must wonder
why in so much creating the great
maker did not predict flaws. there
are places I know God forgot like
the blackout in the city when the
Pentecostals in the building rushed
into the corridors yelling the end
has come, or the time three members
of the Turban Taps gang stomped Rudy
bloody for daring to quit, or the day
Rufina lost a husband and four kids
to soldiers who learned to use American-
made guns to kill for the sake of the Cold
War, and Joey grieving for his mother who
died of pneumonia too poor to live. I do
apologize to pastors, priests, theologians
and pew warmers but there are just too many
places God is nowhere to be seen. I am
more concerned about people not loved and
talked about with language that nails them
figuratively and often physically to trees.
sometimes, we need a bigger name than God
to understand and overcome the fetish for
material things and the sorrow that declares
God is dead!

LOST BOY

I held a stranger's hand who
exited apartment 5C in tears
that had completely drenched
her red blouse. I did not want
to ask any questions and joined
her mindfulness exercise of
hurt until after lighting up the
dark she stared into her empty
apartment saying, I forgot the
sound of my dead son's voice
and I could not remember how
tall he was. she had been folding
a pair of blue jeans that still had
the boy's smell, taking down a
jigsaw puzzle from a wall held
together by scotch tape of the
Adam's Family and switching
on a lamp made by her son in metal
shop screwed into a wall surface. I
could not help thinking her tears on
the hallway floor said haggling with
God was pointless. we walked the
five flights down to the stoop of the
building sat down facing the street
overlooked by heaven and I listened
to the woman share more than a few
lines of her everlasting sadness.

PEACE

the unbearable wailing familiar
to me in the inner city and the
war-torn villages south of the
border break the lines inked on
the pages of the books gathering
dust on shelves that never pick
up the pieces of the forsaken. I
have listened to these cries from
Golgotha, the silence it too often
delivered in the places my beloved
poor mourn, and have stopped trying
to hold back the tears that visit me
when darkness feels too long. if you
come to visit me, perhaps you could
tell me about the prayers you have said
that comfort those who weep and hope
to hear a sweet language that is full of
life. sometimes, I ask forgiveness for
crying, the helplessness on disfigured
streets and the shame not felt by patrons
of hate. if you come this way today, I
will sit quietly with watery eyes and
share with you the songs of survivors
who know what peace, justice and love
brings.

THE MESSIAH

for hundreds of years, they have
prayed in case the Messiah comes
to say something about the unhallowed
use of God on earth. you can easily tell
in the neighborhoods where people cling
like drunks to the world shouting peace
for nothing, or in the experiences in cities
full of churches leaving even the faithful
with more worries, or on the faces of the
poor battered by doubt that there will ever
be a second coming. just once the wretched
of the earth would like to visit a cathedral
to hear a sermon about being sick and tired
of waiting, disapproval about the long delay
across the earth from the visitor from heaven
and no more bending truth pretending that is
God's word. at least today, we want to hold
on to the idea change is coming and pray for
pastors and priests to say something about people
mowed down while the treasurers in churches
make deposits. last night on the stoop there was
talk about faith lost over the next century and I
wondered about the twisted theology that does
not explain why it seems the Messiah has quit
on earth.

THE POETS

I paid attention to the Nuyorican
poets on the Lower East Side who
with simple words told stories of
life kicked aside uptown in temples
of wealth serving bony lobster to dinner
guests. their noisy banging of Spanglish
spilling from unwanted Black and Brown
mouths were other voices gasping for the
blocks trying to beat all the broken English
odds. I recall sitting one night on a barstool
in the poet's café gently laughing with Pietri
about our beloved people playing numeritos
and hoping for the big win that would deliver
them from misfortune. I confessed my mother
used to send me to the corner barbershop to find
Junior who ran numbers on the block and play
five bucks that I thought was too much money
for a family eating once in every while welfare
department cheese. I could never get enough of
an evening with these overlooked poets who
opened their mouths in a wooden-floored room
to say everything is wrong in the country that
cannot hang enough of us. I will never forget
talking to my dear friend Miguel Piñero about
his play *Short Eyes* then playing at the Public
Theater about a white middle-class child molester
thrown into prison with Black and Latino inmates
and all the truth-telling in it that hurt. damn, I

said these malefactors and hard substances make
us ask where do our fucken dreams go and Pietri
said we pass them along hermanito on Avenue D.

THE WORD

the words caught me by surprise
when they arrived in the warming
morning to add to the many sounds
of summer. I could not quite make
out the whispered advice given to the
unbound wind and the Holy silence
waking from rest. I put a finger over
my lips hoping to touch these words
going into the world saying you exist
in the bare rooms of Spanglish. I looked
at the bodies starting to move across
the sidewalk, the many-colored faces,
bells ringing in the Saint Cyril Church
and wondered will they chime in heaven
like they make noise today for us? little
mute Danny who came an undocumented
refugee of war, learned to sign with thin
hands in a language only known by his
mother, joined me on the stoop with a
smile and we leaned into time without
saying a thing.

EVIL

the wickedness around me
makes me shiver about the
good undone. today, I appeal
for you to stand against it
decrying the foul offences.
evangelicals who rushed to
defend a man found guilty in
a court of law of sexual battery
need to be reminded justice matters
on every page of scripture and in
the name of gospel truth. woe to
you embracing racism, misogyny,
the criminalization of immigrants,
the glorification of white violence and
theological pretensions about a white-
only heaven. I say to you who stand
in Lafayette Park with an imbecile who
posed with an upturned Bible the day
of the Lord will be harshness for you
without end. woe to you who follow
each other deeper into ignorance, closer
to hate and away from the lynched God
who answers the knocks on heaven's old
doors.

THE DRUNK

we were used to seeing Shorty on
the block sitting on the stoop across
the street from the Perez grocery store
sipping from a quart bottle of beer
and joking with the little kids going
to school. often, you could hear him
say in a low-voiced prayer Our father
who art in heaven I am getting drunk
and hope that by the middle of this new
day you give me something to eat like
you never forgot to do when I was eight
and working on the corner shining shoes
for a buck. Our God wherever you happen
to be thank you for keeping me out of the
drunk ward at Lincoln Hospital, the local
precinct jail where I was beaten bloody in
my teens, for keeping me in school for 9
good years, allowing me to visit the Bronx
Zoo when a kid, for letting the sickly trees
in the little conga park go on living and for
letting me lurch forth each day alive with a
prayer. Lord, recall that day Shorty was visited
by a group of little kids who sat with him after
jumping double-Dutch rope and he told them
with his stumbling Spanglish tongue I saw
heaven in your skipping feet. Vaya!

LOVE

we sat on wooden chairs in
the quiet café on the Lower East
Side telling tales about crossing
the border and walking curved
streets. we touched hands admitting
the world was too dark for this love,
smiling about a song playing on the
speaker hidden in a corner of the
room and recalling the damp grass
in a Mesoamerican valley reflecting
the flickering stars. if that night was
only a dream, it has made a difference
to matter in the world, and with it I
will continue floating until the wind
cries out you again are coming to me
with your dark pretty face to whisper
into my ear more riotous stories to keep
me from sleep.

THE PREACHER

the preacher with his booming
voice takes the pulpit with a freshly
starched shirt, scientifically pressed
trousers and sparkling new shoes to
talk about the plight of the poor on
God's big earth. the shouts from
the meek of the earth gather outside
his fancy words in all the places evil-
doers twist to do their thing. inside
the sanctuary unfamiliar with swelling
numbers listeners are rarely persuaded to
do a damn thing save compose another
prayer for the regularly forgotten that are
not invited to experience the sweet comforts
of heaven. for all that talk in the polished
wood pulpit the congregants have a way of
knowing how to do little to nothing at all
for those who suffer. when time to leave,
the holy book left on the altar is picked at
by vultures who do not give a damn about
God.

CIVIL WAR

I feel asleep on a hammock
drifting in and out of vague
dreams where tongues came
out of the earth on the bloody
civil war field speaking peace
in shouts. I felt in it afraid of
love dying on earth and God
silent. I tossed about trapped in
the groaning dream, crying for
dead relatives and old friends,
shouting at the delusions of Mass
and unable to escape suffering.
irregular voices began talking to
me clearer than all the stacked
books in the church with the cross
arrested by soldiers and judged
subversive, these voices spoke
of unforgettable things and called
for the resurrection of peace.

CROTONA PARK

after the weeks of wandering to get
here they tumbled into Crotona Park
full of flowers, grassy meadows, and
rising granite. the mothers sat on old
benches with tears in their brown eyes
for children at play, sharing stifled
memories of a foreign land where the
poor are scorned, eating Milk Duds for
a first time and saying prayers about
how to forgive the wicked. they had
new lives in the Bronx waiting with
others in crowded apartments to feel
a Holy presence driving away regrets.
they heard fire sirens rushing down Tremont
Avenue breaking the silence of home altars
for Saints to whom nightly they offered
petitions. today, together in the park
they managed to forget why they fled El
Salvador and in the moment could not
keep from giving thanks to God, friends
and the long walk that brought them to
a safer place.

PROUD MARY

in the summer of 1969, a lunar
module landed on the moon for
two men to take a giant step they
said for those on earth, the Fifth
Dimension was singing the Age
of Aquarius, Nixon became the
37th president of the States, guns
flashed in a hideous Vietnam war,
Puerto Rican boys and girls in the
barrio were shooting Southeast Asian
dope and Tina sang a song about a woman
who gets off the bus to work for the rich
called "Proud Mary." who can forget the
Black and Brown bodies stumbling in
the American dark, dancing at all the
block parties, going to school with slim
odds, joining the Marine Corp to get away
from the block and coming back in body
bags to keep the Ortiz Funeral Home in
business. Tito told me that summer there
is a song for every occasion, to lift hearts
and make us protest for peace.

DEMENTIA

on another day, you returned
to the city to your aging mother's
place in the projects on Avenue
D, the doctor you talked to said
she is aware though uncertain of
her capacity to remember your
face and name. you went to the
church on Sunday with memories
that crawled out of bed with smiles
for your mother who loses her place
too easily, keeps a Bible next to her
bed though one page to her is now no
different than any other. we walked
back to the apartment that afternoon,
you misty eyed and telling me it is
best not to ask her to understand or
remember and perhaps we should
spend the time just holding your
dear mother's hand, saying a few
prayers, confessing her illness will
not speak and loving the old woman
until the God Lord declares she is
done.

SOFA BED

in the living room of the
apartment once lived by
orthodox Jews sheltering
in the Bronx, I slept in a
sofa bed with my brother
we pulled out each night
with Jesus whispering to us
from the altar in the next
room that mother kept in
light with candles. nightly
we studied the usefulness
of sleep with long talks into
the widening darkness that
dissolved into dreams of no
use whatsoever when it was
time to get up for the walk
to public school. one late
Fall night we had the oddest
identical dream that the living
room was invaded by desperate
Day of the Dead skeletons that
woke us up yelling they are no
longer dying of hunger but had
unquenchable thirst from the long
journey to see us. we did not
have bread to give them and too
few memories to leave in a corner
of the room for them. I recall looking

into my brother's eyes in that time the
veil was thin enough for these uninvited
creatures to show up and followed him in the
act of wrestling skeletons to leave them
with the unmistakable conclusion these
Puerto Rican boys were unafraid to wrestle
with the dead.

MEMORIAL DAY

we make visits to the cemeteries with prayer for those from many ways of life who made the ultimate sacrifice across land and sea for the cause of freedom. they are with us like the caressing breeze of a warm day, the tender leaves on the weeping willows lining the walks at Arlington, memories never forgotten that come unexpectedly to make us stumble in unpracticed steps and in every heaping remain of love in us who stand beside the monuments and graves. now, we whisper that you lived to mark your place on earth, while a bugle summons us once again to tears for the price you paid with tattered flags flying in bloody conflicts to inch us closer to liberty and peace. in God's earth where you have come to rest you will find us telling your story to the world that finds thousands of ways to close its doors on every truth dropped by the fallen into cruel laps.

THE CHEVY

the old man was the first on
the block to buy a brand new
Chevy Impala in burnt brown
that he came out to drive with a
cap. on rides to Orchard Beach
every window came down, three
kids in the back seat wrestled and
his wife who arrived from a little
village in Puerto Rico leaned into
him waving at the Jewish couple
sitting in their spot on the sidewalk
on beach chairs. you could see by
the white in his eyes that he burned
with perfection that exploded by the
second bigger than the sun following
him to the beach, where he would tell
anyone of the fine car a policeman's
salary permitted him. the kids on the
block made sure nothing happened to
the Chevy of this man they knew by the
name Johnny the cop. once upon a time,
he was just another Puerto Rican boy who
graduated Monroe High School though he
grew older listening to heavy thumping in
his soft heart.

SUBWAY RIDE

enough time had passed since I
saw you for the first time carrying
a message written on a piece of
cardboard as you walked distances
in subway cars. the first time I saw
you was on the IRT #2 line, after the
Harlem riots when King was killed,
blind in one eye and asking riders to
share a little change for the rent due
next month, surgery for the other eye
and help for an ill mother. you mastered
the balanced walk through the cars,
smiled at artfully dressed riders and
caught glimpses of your face in the
plexiglass windows that popped up like
an unexpected pigeon from a magician's
hat. seeing you making the rounds after
so many years, an expert in the familiar
dark of tunnels, the sickish struggle of
dreams, and sinking into the deep well
of subway riders' indifference left me
weeping like Sancho who could not hold
back tears for languishing Don Quixote.
at the end of the ride, I had to whisper
in your ear forgive us for looking away
from the history you drag by the ankles
on a train posted with signs warning its
unlawful to spit.

THE BEGINNING

the shadows, the streets, the old country widows, the church choirs, children skipping rope, and local park preachers shouting about the open gates of heaven are hinted by the rubble in the empty lots and the bricks holding up our souls. on this block that yearned for the great feasts of faith without judgement, stories are still found written on the foot bridges leading to the East River in the park where stray dogs roam and winos drink to accuse bitter days. the candles are burning in churches, apartment altars full of Saints, in alleys junkies use to shoot up dope and places in the barrio where Spanglish lips pray to see God just once. there are no signs of life on the block for the suffering and the tired have managed to escape, some even to parts of the city where the shameless of the nation sleep.

HEAL

I have been told to talk with
someone about the dreadful
feelings of grief that draped
me like a veil the night my
brother stopped living. that
evening which became part
of the written history of my
Puerto Rican soul never stops
weeping. I dare say professionals
paid to listen would not find
me in their rooms and nothing
said would blow a single speck
of dust from the dry leaves still
in me since that Fall twilight of
my brother's end. you may agree
time does not heal wounds, it lets
you endure them, talk with them like
unwanted visitors and call out to
God in the bareness. I have been
told to let go, but such words will never
lead me away from the beautiful and
precious recollections of a brother
who in my sorrowing heart exists like
a hidden treasure so familiar to the boys
and girls skipping on New York City
streets.

LA PLACITA

in the placita I never visited
with mother, there was years
ago a public television around
which people gathered to view
American shows in Spanish. I
grew up watching action shows
in the park, sleeping the long night
on its benches, telling myself the
homeless and hungry waited for
a slice of Wonder bread with the
patient pigeons. I was an expert
at doing without, being put to the
test by dark times and talking in
the local cathedral to Saints. one
afternoon roaming the streets asking
tourists to spare a little change, a
white girl smiled and gave me a few
quarters asking to touch my hair. I
supposed my Puerto Rican natural
peeked her interest to step into the
territory that for me was a tale of
a different life.

THE SHORE

I sat on the banks of the Atlantic sea, cotton ball clouds floated above, the fragrance of flowers held long enough by the passing breeze for notice, a pair of pelicans diving for fish like they have for ages and sounds of everything alive playing in the eager day. I sat to think of the morning views older than this turning earth, a river in the mountains 45 million years old, the underground caves it carved for miles and deep into the souls that see. my ancestors bathed in these waters before the arrival of Spanish tongues, they were lulled into sleep by its singing current and the sweet mysteries it held. I sat for hours by the ocean shore thinking of the limitless sky, the ancient river running for the sea, throaty waves making land and imagining in many ways the bejeweled reveries of Taínos and Africans unchained.

IMAGO DEI

we are made in the image of God
in a world divided by madness. we
try to breathe and move in it to make
things whole. we wonder who are
those who never stepped on the bottom
rung of a ladder to heaven? some of us
question too those churches telling us
you have the right to remain silent and
any Spanish you dare speak will make
a white God stutter. what prayer won't
fix is the blue-eyed image of Christ on
these church windows and the lesser
imago dei imagined by congregations
that think they have a right to speak
in the name of Christ who died like
we do every damn day in the color
of white sin. we may spend the late
Sunday afternoon singing the same
hymns but no matter how you interpret
your Holy book the Crucified carpenter
knows us like the wickedness that nailed
him to a lynching tree.

TORN FABRIC

a hole was torn in the narrative
of national birth, the story line
unraveled by the people closest
to the words of biblical prophets
who have made it their business
to probe for truth. no one expected
the days to be counted by the tears
of the poor, the slaughtered, raped
and lynched nor the vast other story
to be written. the fabric is ripped
today by those who know time is
a slow-moving train taking them to
the place of deliverance remembering
themselves in ways never discussed
or written in authorized history. the
hole grows bigger each day to allow
people with no clear view of themselves
to squeeze through to get a view of the
olden times that fell from grace since the
beginning. the torn open hole was found
in my beloved slum in the middle of a
lot that misplaced Chico's tenement that
everyone thought is not the country. the
little kids have touched it up with graffiti
and I suspect it will be reported in the next
few weeks on an episode of the Discovery
Channel introducing the Fall.

SCHOOL DAYS

each day the long walk to
school was like the previous
one. waking up to sounds
from a kitchen radio delivering
news from a world thousands
of miles away in a language
the teachers at school did not
understand, discussing with Joey
how the color of the sky on Spring
mornings was no less blue than
the home room teacher's eyes and
practicing arguments to toss out
during the classes that conveniently
left too many sides of history out
of morning lessons. the walk produced
thoughts we did not know existed
in us like talking our way through
the country trying to slam the door on
our faces, inventing Spanglish curses
for bitter sentences stuffed by America
down our sofrito throats and standing
on long lines after school for a free
meal made by loving old Jewish ladies'
hands with ingredients unknown to a
Spanish-speaking God who listened to the
spoken prayers of the illiterate mothers
raising us.

LOCKED

the church door was locked
like every day save Sunday
keeping me from lighting a
candle to Nuestra Señora de
Guadalupe and kneeling to
pray. I longed for the cool
feel of the narthex, to dip a
finger in Holy Water, to take
in whatever Spirits lurked in
the sanctuary and even to get
a look at her watching from the
altar made by Irish immigrants
the junkies who were not blind
to the Crucified God in people
around them. I wanted God to
speak, for shouts of amen to come
through cracked wood, for anyone
to walk by the bolted church speaking
in tongues. after a thirty-minute wait,
Hector came my way to assure me
the church bells only ring backwards
and nothing gets in or out of that stoned
house of worship. I walked away with
Hector suggesting we go to the corner
to wait for the One who leads the way
to heaven.

CHURCH OF ALL NATIONS

I was invited to a dinner party in a
posh neighborhood by people who said
in the middle of the meal, you are
not like the others. a chill and loss
of words took over to remind me as
a young pastor that nothing in the world
can equal the horror of living with utter
ignorance. wine circulated the table, the
laughter flowed and I fixed my eyes on
a spot on the wall thinking about a sad
God. it was the very first time I was a
wined and dined spic with the fashionably
rich though not the last with the righteously
stupid. the host looked across the table at
me saying in a polite sort of way I don't
speak Spanish, so I shared English is a second
language for me and I use it to translate mother's
perfect Spanish and especially when listening to
the distant songs pouring into an intolerant world
from heaven. what I wanted to feel was not at the
dinner table nor the polite conversation, instead it
was on the Lower East Side and in my ordinary
Spanish-speaking church in laborious pain trying
to give birth to a different life.

THE SNEAKERS

a summer morning seeped
into Spanish Harlem blowing
a warm breeze across the face
of the priest wearing a Roman
collar with Nike sneakers. the
flock of tourists packed into a
passing bus pushed cameras out
of open windows to photograph
whatever moved and the housing
projects built on the ruins from a
time of conquest. the elderly who
have felt life too small look out of
windows thinking there is so much
to miss each day, the riding tourists are
foreigners and they will forget this visit
like frayed leaves cast off in Autumn by
by sickly Central Park trees. the hotline
for troubled Puerto Rican youth was in
a project tenement with high school kids
handling calls and never mentioning the
absent God. twice a week I listened to
other kids held captive to bag dope and
a lengthy history of being done wrong. I
hugged callers with aching words and did
my best to keep the lights on. I confess
like Spanish Harlem they live in the knots
in my throat.

THE LIVING

tears catch me by surprise
like rain, unexpected. since
the day I put you in God-made
earth, they make their way to
me with memories that dance
around the puddles. I have no
way of explaining why for these
many years this happens though
the sadness makes sense when I
pray to remember the sound of
your voice. I have waited more
than three decades to find a way
beyond my grief, to push it beyond
darkness, to feel heaven turning it
to laughter, but dear brother I must
tell you the last tear that fell to the
sidewalk helped me to understand
missing you is God's gift. I have
learned to hear you speak in the
silence, in my pumping Spanish-
speaking heart and recalling the
ways you smuggled love into the
world of the poor, rejected and
forgotten.

THE PROFESSOR

the theology professor was a figure
in the classroom for more than fifty
years undoing white-washed thoughts
about God and removing misleading
signs in the church. students flocked
to his courses to get a glimpse at his
reverence for mystery and to listen to
remarkable soliloquies about the light
surrounding a Jewish man who for sin
was lynched and remade white. I was
among those who sat in the classroom
eager for a Black God to descend from
heaven to invite my dear professor to
sit for a ride in the ancient chariot that
set us free. I recall certain winter nights
walking the city streets disordered by
sirens, beeping horns and unidentifiable
tones how beautiful to think of the divine
apart from the theological certitudes of a
twitchy faith that believes the Word of
the Almighty for stomped human beings
is heaven will make it up to you. the theology
professor nurtured this stubborn singing in
me each time he talked with his feet on the
ground challenging the authoritarian nature
of the white God-makers who sold too many
of us structured feelings and traditions that
tossed aside the poor dark-skinned carpenter
from the ratty side of town.

SUNDAY

Sundays in the barrio I got up
early while others slept to polish
my single pair of dress shoes and
wear fine threads to make my way
to kids' Mass. I was never sure about
hearing some new truth about living
poor in the city. the Irish and Italian
immigrant priests did not point out the
signs to make us believe in a coming
day when the cool air of prosperity would
find us in the tenements and underpaid
work. I simply attended services to
pray to the heavenly mute overlooking
the block where childhood dreams were
kicked into nightmares. I sat in the pews
with young devout souls in the barrio and
Sunday became a time to again hear in the
beginning was the word, to see the light of
heaven shine on brown faces and to place
Spanglish in the hands of grace. Sunday
was that day of the week the kids gathered
in the old brick church to shout holy, holy,
holy Mother of God pray for us here today
and gone tomorrow.

PARSIFAL

ordinary time is magical by the
second when you open your eyes
to see it, I concluded while leaving
Lincoln Center following a viewing
of *Parsifal* on a Good Friday. I walked
South on Broadway in the company of
a friend who wore a thin gold necklace
with a cross who asked what do you want
to do now? I thought it was a good night
for a long walk on city sidewalks with the
people Jesus redeemed, to hold hands in
the journey like they were the hem of a
divine garment and realize that no matter
how many decades have passed ultimate
meaning evades language like Proteus. I
recall it felt good to walk after the rather
long Wagner opera on that cool night and
feeling saved by the power of shared words
in an evening stroll. on that extraordinary
night, I walked feeling closer to the reach
of grace. we ambled by an old man playing
the violin for the public filling the air with
miraculous notes that drifted the length of
the street like they were played with strands
from the bow on Elijah's violin.

DAWN

the slumbrous morning in rising light is kissed awake by Angels on fire escapes. the eye can see night is done for a fresh day to speak in any and every language. longing hearts meet the nascent brightness without gloom and in the name of a mystifying gospel that will sink deep in us. like a vaporous mist rising the side of mountains to heaven each soul welcomes this astonishing thing called life.

LOOKING

I went outside looking for
you despite being told the
soldiers would shoot me.
only your tenderness could
make me tremble and your
face I expected to appear
fair and your hand warm to
the touch. every evening you
placed flowers on the altar of
the Holy Mother so I went there
to look for you and waited for
the winds of heaven to lead me
to your side. when I found you
the last army trucks were leaving
the Colonia and I embraced your
unharmed body more certain that
I belonged to you then and for the
questioned eternity to come.

WITNESS

I have walked behind you
muttering about the mysteries
of heaven in a crippled world.
sometimes I do not even know
what to believe, where to look
for signs or what time to admit
myself a stranger on this earth
nature keeps occupied. perhaps,
you think my footsteps are too
far behind you to hear or living
in the slum and experiencing the
bloodshed of civil war left me a
willing subject of apostasy. over
the years, I have visited the places
where others keep company with
you in more than prayer, acting in
light of their hope for life without
cruelty and untimely death, yet I
confess these followers and even
martyrs loved you deeper than the
weeping in the world allows me to
know. though I follow you from
time to time at a distance tell me
it is true that silence recalls your
presence entangled in us.

MASS

the apartments emptied for Sunday
Mass permitting silence to break
into the corridors children normally
played. the air hanging around the
block came from another place to
talk Spanish to loud cheers like the
times family arrived after weeks of
walking North. candles light faces
of Saints in the tenement homes to
warm simple altars and the hearts of
those who carried them, prayed with
them, and gave thanks to each of them
for making it through shivering nights
after weeks of walking. the little alley
where stray dogs whimper is the shortest
way to the place where old Ave Marias
are said recalling the living, the dead and
martyred. after church, folks with acquired
names take meals in the basement with Irish
and Italian priests sitting at tables sharing
funny stories beneath the constant watch
of Nuestra Señora de Guadalupe standing
in a corner of the room. odd how there
are Saints from the North, others from
the South and the Holy Mother changes
names.

THE BLUES

sometimes, when the sun goes down
low enough you can feel the blues in
your rickety soul and find comfort in
the soft-spoken notes of Chet Baker
singing "My Funny Valentine." sometimes,
listening to Chet's nearly whispered
lyrics and smooth trumpet leaves your
melancholy robed in purple. sometimes,
the blues hold on more stubbornly than
the Sunday gospel poured into clay jar
lives and you remember tales from way
back when that make you wonder why.
sometimes, when I was strung out people
with a dictatorial faith said I was going to
hell. sometimes, I felt brittle as a twig
and knew God must be laughing at the
idea of sending me to a place of burning
fires and evil eyed creatures for being a
junkie boy full of blues especially when
in the big world Christians kill Christians
in the blessed One's name. sometimes, I
think there is nothing like letting the blues
hold me close and Chet buzzing the dozens
of doorbells deep down in me.

SAGE

she understood the meaning of
offering prayer for the deceased,
creating beauty saying the Rosary
in memory of a sister, the promises
offered by Saints and martyrs of a
coming time of peace and future of
reunion. everyone took note of the
presence of the Holy Mother in the
white sage smoke drifting about the
room cleansing their souls, they spoke
the blessings of smoke in prayer and
with sacred words created life again
from death. no one talked about the
day of crying their lungs out, tumbling
into months-long silence, questioning
the idea of finding life in Christ and
believing in the resurrection. the time
was devoted to the sacred Mother who
led them where healing was most needed
as well as waiting for the one who oddly
is forever on his way. although I cannot
fully surrender to the Rosary prayer beads
made by the Indian hands from the land
that is sacred to me I confess being led by
the pious habit to the love that proposes
nothing more than blessed memories and
life.

WASHINGTON SQUARE

like the lovers on the grass in
Washington Square Park on a
Summer evening you made on
another land sat on the slanted
park bench with wood from what
seemed a different century counting
their kisses in Spanish. the lamp-lights
placed around the square cracked all
darkness, dogs played merry games
with children, occasionally sparrows
floated over the fountain in the middle
of the park and your fingers tightened
in my hand as you placed your naked
feet in its cooling water. that evening
was life beyond any imagined depth
and felt with a simplicity that permitted
us to imagine the pool of water collected
in the fountain an ocean shining on the
earth. I loved the way the faint city
lights fell over the park and how a breeze
brushed hair away from your eyes making
us blush at once with contentment and a
future that was utterly free.

THE CROSSING

when you live across the border
it means the wind blows daily in
the wrong direction, you are not
sure whether you are coming or
going, you hear people shout go
back to your country though you
were born right here, your Spanish-
speaking mother gives you an English
name, and you spend time searching
for the Indian, African and Spaniard
for centuries inside you silent. to live
in the place across the river means
recalling the mango tree you planted
with your grandmother, almost sense
the bittersweet aroma of dandelions
pushing through grass on the Catholic
schoolyards, see elderly fathers walking
down the hill from a cathedral that still
weeps for its martyrs and hear the old
cashew tree saying your northern name
with the sweetest accent. when you live
on this side of the border people look at you
doubly and though you are home most do
not want you to stay. no one understands
you were brought into this world in a city
hospital by a peasant mother who could
not have you in her own unsafe land so
thoroughly owned by Uncle Sam's aging
empire.

CRUEL THING

in her country that has ripped holes
in the ground for more years than
remembered, she was a university
student until forced to escape death
by coming to the United States. she
passed the Catholic school on the way
to the first border crossing where she
laughed with friends, made it after many
setting suns to the other riverbank, arrived
in a city founded long ago by an English
colony and found off-the-books work caring
for someone else's children, cleaning homes
on Saturday and claiming Sunday for herself
to feel closer to the God who seems to have
forgotten the abysmal land she fled. I see her
daily living without making a sound, telling her
story now and then to the deaf, praying in an
English-speaking cathedral and staring at the
Saints without Spanish names who appear to
have time to listen. one Sunday, kneeling at
the altar rail I could faintly hear her request
for God to clean up history and help everyone
recall how it was when no one was left with the
unwelcome task of cleaning bloody rags or dealing
with the rubbish heap of arguments justifying hell
on earth.

BUTTERFLY

how hot it is on this bright
summer day with crickets
jumping in the grass and
tiny lizards scratching the
dirt. a glass of ice-water
melts on the wood stump
table and I sit to eavesdrop
on birds. a monarch butterfly
arrives flapping about I imagine
after crossing mountains, border
walls, rivers and boundaries on
the way likely to Michoacan. she
pauses on bright yellow flowers,
waits for a little while and takes
to the air again never stumbling
in her long journey. she like me
is a speck in the universe and I
whisper a message for her to carry
for the many miles she must travel
before sleep. the little creature is
a migrant with no name, no passport,
no past tense words and driven by a
southern destination. I say goodbye
to her in graceful flight asking the little
friend to tell the gods along the way to
find me and all the weary in this English-
speaking town.

INDICTMENT

how many ways can a
man scream innocent with
his hand caught directing
the move of boxes filled with
classified secrets captured on
film? how much money can
a man who devastated the nation
make from multiple indictments
to satisfy his greed? how many
citizens will keep looking away
from the man who makes a living
piling up lies while wrapped in a
soiled flag? I have listened to the
silent stones speak while the dark
made its way to light, louder than
the man who faced terror on the
wood of the tree, stuttering at the
slanted scales of two-timing law,
and occasionally murmuring odd
noises when MAGA lynch-mobs turn
corners to murder the truth without
remorse. gather round for the stones
told me there is hardly anyone left in
the church who believes it possible to
die for the truth!

WORD

in the apartment shared with
a dozen others a single mattress
claims space on a floor called
your room. a light bulb hangs
shining yellow from a string in
the old place and you stare at it
nights thinking about praying for
forgiveness though you have not
figured out what debt. some nights
drunken voices from another crowded
chamber lighten the space with Spanish
words, stories about living thirsty in
a foreign culture and being swallowed
up each day at work and spat out with
English curses. you rise each morning
to make your way to the subway station
with sighing eyes that tell more than you
have ever spoken and with desert dust
still lodged in them. you have existed
now on the fringes of this new world
for nearly five years and the sidewalk
cracks have learned to say your name
more than seminary trained preachers
expecting to be paid for sermons.

THE SUBWAY

I hear the subway squeaking
down the tracks past the
unmarked graves of the dead
from poverty and dope that
have flowers placed on them
each week. the names knotting
my throat fall into the night in
mourning and I want to rush
downstairs to take a long walk
on the sidewalk to find the Holy
abuelas with prayers for us. I fall
to my knees for the sake of those
called sinners by priests though I
shouted a list of disagreements to
heaven. the psalmist's words come
to me, the Lord is my shepherd, I
shall not want, the Lord guides me
by the East River, but with brothers
and sisters in this slum I keep waiting
for God's block to have a little more
life and far less of the most high's
silence and darkness.

CHUCK

we will remember you in
prayer for kindness with
the gentlest smiles in this
time of disbelief for your
crossing into a place of
silence. we will remember
you in the passing seconds
in these halls in which family,
friends and students will weep
and for days on end trying to absorb
the mystery of your sudden exit.
we will remember talking while
breaking bread, memories shared
about what mattered great and
small, the hours spent in Chapel
reverence, the first time you preached
in Spanish, the seasons of life known
with you counted today among our
cherished blessings. we will remember
your faith that led us quietly to light,
counted death as nothing at all and
that will meet us with laughter when
the time comes for us to meet once
again.

THE CORNERSTONE

the fiendish mob cast
its eyes on the ghastly
body left to swing by
the impenitent lynchers
who delighted with dreadful
throngs that came to gaze
without a single tear at the
terror of white sin. the young
Black man named William
Allen Taylor, was taken from
this world with cruelest hate,
his woe one last September day
thickened hearts with grief and
the sorrow of a long-suffering
people. today, I confess once
the cornerstone was unveiled
I prayed for every lyncher in
God's world to be swallowed
into hell.

www.ingramcontent.com/pod-product-compliance
Lightning Source LLC
Chambersburg PA
CBHW062222080426
42734CB00010B/1989